Surviving a War Enduring the Peace

A Child's Life During WW-2 and the Ensuing Allied Occupation

Remembered by Klaus O. Staerker

ISBN:13 9781711755861

DEDICATION

This book is based on the experiences of one child. I dedicate it to the memory of one and a half million children who cannot tell their stories because they perished during World War Two. Some of these children could have been my playmates, but they were killed because they either were born to parents hated by Adolph Hitler, or they fell victims to the bombs of their liberators. Klaus speaks for them.

ACKNOWLEDGMENTS

Martha J. Martin

Without her personal interest, friendship and publishing expertise, my story would remain a secret.

Table of Contents

DEDICATION......I

ACKNOWLEDGMENTS......II

FORWORD......V

THREE YEARS OF PEACE......8

THE WAR STARTS......13

A HARBINGER OF THE AIR WAR......16

THE FIGHTING COMES HOME......19

AIR RAIDS AND INCREASING DANGER......23

THE ALLIES' JUSTIFICATION FOR BOMBINGS......27

WAR ON THE HOME FRONT......30

PROPAGANDA BRAIN WASHING MISINFORMATION.32

CHILDREN'S EVACUATION TO SAFETY......37

LIFE IN FOSTER CARE......39

THE AIR WAR EXPANDS......43

A HAPPY FOSTER HOME......49

MY LAST SIX MONTHS IN AUSTRIA......51

THE BEGINNING OF THE END......58

REIGN OF TERROR......64

THE NUMBERS BEHIND THE RAIDS......71

ESCAPE FROM HELL......74

A TEMPORARY HOME IN SAFETY......76

1945 – THE END IS NEAR......80

THE START OF FOREIGN OCCUPATION......83

DAD'S HOMECOMING......90

LIFE AS A FAMILY 93
ENDURING THE PEACE 95
RETURN TO NOTHING 98
A NEW NORMAL 106
PICKING UP THE PIECES 108
A NEW WEAPON – DEMOLITION 111
SCHOOLS OPEN AGAIN 112
ECONOMIC SURVIVAL 115
DEATH RETURNED 122
JOY OF A RADIO 124
GIFTS FROM AMERICA 126
DAD'S STRUGGLE 128
AMERICA'S MASSIVE AID 130
LIFE SLOWLY RETURNS TO NORMAL 134
BIG STEP TO ADULTHOOD 137
AFTEREFFECTS 140
PREPARATION FOR A NEW LIFE 144
A NEW WORLD 146
EPILOGUE 148

FORWORD

In the Summer of 2017, I gave two short talks to the WW-2 Military Historical Society in Ashland, Kentucky, about my WW-2 and post-war experiences: "Surviving the War" and "Enduring the Peace".

For years, Nellie Staerker, my wife, had urged me to write about those experiences. I was not interested, because my story is like that of millions of others, and it had been very difficult for me to talk about those days. Bill Martin, one of the active members of the Ashland Heritage Museum, approached me right after my talk. "You must write a book about your life in WW-2 Germany." A week later, I received a call from Dave Payne, another attendee of that program, "You must write a book.".

Both men emphasized the fact that most war-related books are about experiences by adults, written by adults; there is little told by children. The reasoning made me realize that the book would not just be about me: it would be a book paralleling the experiences of millions of children, told by one child – one that lived to tell his version – one small voice in the chorus of victims of global violence.

Countless children suffered far more than I did, but I can only tell what happened to me, an average child, and what happened to me was often very unpleasant. It took many decades to be able to talk in detail about that part of my life. The realization about the severity of the past has resulted in a few tears and many sleepless nights, and I now realize how much worse the time was then it seemed when I was in the thick of it. I suffered from PTSD seventy-five years ago, long before it was recognized; it robbed me of peaceful sleep and affected my daily life. Most of it has left me, but some of it will always linger in my mind.

Writing this book has been therapeutic for me. Yes, some of the awakened memories are painful to me, but I have dealt with that pain, and my mind is better off; the suffering is over. I live a good life.

While I was writing this book, I read “One Step Ahead of Hitler,” by Fred Gross, a Jewish survivor of Hitler's “Final Solution Plan,” and I almost scrapped my ideas to write. My experiences pale in comparison to Fred's, but then I realized that we are not competing for setting records in life's miseries – we are just telling our stories.

The end of the war could not be the end of my story, because the struggle for physical survival had been replaced by an economic struggle – a peace time extension of a shooting war –

one without bullets and bombs. The new weapons were food, clothing, and shelter, more precisely: the absence and scarcity of what people needed to live a reasonably normal life

Many names, places, and dates have faded out of my memory, but the main events are still as clear as they were when they happened. All of my close family members have passed on, and I have no one to ask for details, but I remember enough to represent a picture that will give you a good understanding of what life was like for many children in Hitler's Germany – miserable and uncertain.

Everything you will read here is based on facts; there is no fiction and no embellishment to generate entertainment. What you will read is the echo of my past. While I don't have the words to effectively convey to you all the powerful emotions of those terrible years, I think you will get the general idea.

THREE YEARS OF PEACE

My first three years of life were normal for that age. A child cannot discern the political turmoil of the military preparations for world domination attempts. The next six years were different; they were turbulent for all Germans; they affected the rest of my life. What did I do to deserve the hardship? Nothing on my part, other than I was born to German parents. I certainly did not cause that, but I was fortunate that both parents were of proper government approved German heritage.

Everything remotely connected to morals and human decency was turned upside down. The government dictated what was appropriate to say, hear, and see. My country had become an artificial and evil empire – individuals no longer mattered.

I came into this World on May 14, 1936, in Duisburg, Germany. Duisburg is located at the Western end of the Ruhr Valley, Germany's industrial center at the Rhine and Ruhr Rivers confluence. It is located about 150 miles from Amsterdam and 400 miles from London. This area is part of the Rhineland that was occupied by the French after World War-1 until Hitler forced them out.

Duisburgers live among four major steel mills, copper and aluminum refineries, heavy equipment manufacturers, and many coal mines. The residents are concentrated around factories.

Most of the houses were dark gray or brown from unabated pollution.

Because of the need to transport massive amounts of products, i.e.: coal, iron ore, and steel, Duisburg has the largest river harbor in the World. Simply stated: Duisburg was one of the most important industrial towns in Germany, especially for war related products.

At the turn of the Century, a large part of the population came from Eastern Europe, especially from Poland, to provide workers for the mills. Because the industry grew with such a rapid pace, there were not enough Germans available to fill the jobs. Still in 1957, there were street vendors with horse-drawn wagons calling out their services in Polish melodic sentences. About 20% of the people in my greater neighborhood seemed to have names ending in “ski”: Podgorski, Kaminski, Majewski, and some had unpronounceable names starting with combinations of “S”, “Z”, and “C.”

My family was typical working class. Dad was the head waiter in the “Casino,” the private hotel owned by the steel giant August Thyssen. He had started his apprenticeship for that occupation an age fourteen, as was the customary path for most trades. He had a respectable job that provided for a comfortable lifestyle. Mom stayed at home to take care of me and my brother, Kurt, born two years earlier than I.

Mom had two brothers, Karl and Willie; they were journeyman machinists at Krupp, Germany's biggest armament factory in Essen, about twenty-five miles from us. Heinz was her sister's husband. In the thirties, he lived near us; he was unemployed. He looked like the model German: tall, blonde, and blue-eyed. He joined the SS, because this was the only job he could find to support his wife and three children. They moved to near Nuremberg in Bavaria. Friedel, Mom's sister, married Bertie, he was a mechanic at Krupp.

Dad's brother Kurt had worked at Krupp to become a pattern maker like his dad; since he was associated with a socialist youth group he was fired as soon as he finished his apprenticeship. In 1924, during the French occupation of the Rhineland, unemployment was high. Uncle Kurt had been blacklisted and could not find work as a craftsman. He worked as collector for a Jewish money lender. In 1957 he still blamed the Jews for causing Germany's problem by lending money at high interest rates. This was a convenient excuse for many Germans to justify the course of history. Kurt did not like Jews and Nazis, and the Nazis did not like Kurt. He left Germany in 1929 to escape Hitler's militia. Several of his friends did not survive the Nazi purges.

Our second story apartment was on Schulstrasse, three blocks from the Casino. My early memories were pleasant. We often played on the hotel grounds and could see Dad at work between meals. His duty required long hours into the night; therefore, home life mostly included Mom, Kurt, and me.

One strong memory was my escape from our house. We were out on the sidewalk when mom stepped inside for a moment. I got out of the stroller and walked the short distance to the Casino. We had gone there many times; therefore, I knew the route. Mom suspected where I went and followed me, but before she got to me, I already had pulled the compact stroller up the hotel steps, and I was standing inside the fancy foyer with a big smile and stinky pants. I was two and a half years old and proud of my achievement. I was always an independent character, and I think that is was one reason for my attraction to America.

The second memorable event in my life was rather traumatic; it was a precursor of life under the control of the Nazis. Kurt and I were playing on the wide sidewalk when we heard the drone of approaching motorcycles. Ten or twelve of them came roaring down the street. The bikes had sidecars attached, and three of them occupied the width of the street. The riders were the dreaded "Brownshirt's," members of the "SA," Hitler's militia.

Our neighbor's twins, aged three, ran into the street cheering and waving their arms; they were excited about the military display, but no one hit the brakes. The first side car slammed into one of the boys and flung him high in the air – then the small convoy stopped. That image is still in my mind. I did not understand why this accident was not avoided. It bothered me for a long time. It was a signal that far worse things were going to happen, but I was too young to recognize it.

We moved to a bigger apartment, three blocks away on Bayreutherstrasse, three hundred meters from a huge coking plant that supplied coke to nine adjacent blast furnaces. We literally lived in the shadows of the blast furnaces. We shared the three-story house with the Winkler family whose oldest son Willie was already in the military service. The younger one, Herman, was serving an apprenticeship at the mill, but his employment ended prematurely when he was drafted into the army, one year before he finished the required training. This practice became common when Germany needed more soldiers than were available at the normal minimum draft age

For a while our life was normal. We had several playmates on our block with a very wide sidewalk next to our house for a playground. One of my close friends, Rosemarie Noetzel, had several highly desirable toys: Lego blocks, roller skates with ball bearings, and a scooter with pneumatic wheels and a treadle to propel it, and she freely shared these toys with us. In early 1939, the "Party", i.e.: N.S.D.A.P, the Nazis, sponsored a carnival party for kids in the Casino. It was fun and games and getting a taste of a beverage that soon disappeared: Coca Cola.

THE WAR STARTS

September 1, 1939 was the day of the surprise attack on Poland. I don't recall the day, at three and a half, war is difficult to understand. However, during the next six years, I lived through many demonstrations that defined war with brutal clarity.

Around that time, Dad's mother came to live with us, and Dad left. In 1957 I learned what had happened. Dad had beaten my Mother severely, and she was in the hospital for nine days. I suspect that Dad had too much alcohol again and lost control. Alcohol was part of his daily life; it was easy to get at work. To avoid legal problems, Dad had joined the Army.

What happened to us during the next six years was impossible to imagine, and some of it is still painful to talk about. I shall try to explain my experiences of that time, not with the words of an historian, but from the memory of an involuntary participant, an innocent child, and tell my version for those who were silenced and cannot tell theirs.

By 1940, I became aware that life was no longer normal. The daily news on the radio was full of war reports; there was little else discussed. The Fatherland's armies were victorious and, of course, justified and right in every way. The propaganda machinery under the leadership of Joseph Goebbels went into overtime and never slowed down.

During the 1940 Easter week, the military base where Dad trained had an open house for families of soldiers. Since the base was located near a small town without hotels, the citizens of that town offered their homes to the visitors. We stayed with the family that owned the popular Circus Althoff. I believe it was their Winter quarters. I watched as the slack rope girls practiced; they worked very hard.

On the base we saw demonstrations of weapons and the rigors of military life. The featured meal was "Eintopf", one-pot. It is a type of stew that contains anything edible. We ate lots of it during the war, because it was easy to fix and could hide the less desirable food items to "stretch" the meal for additional volume.

Our last meal on the base generated a special memory. Mom had ordered strawberry pie for dessert; when the waitress returned, she took the last piece to the next table. I saw that pie about ten feet from me, and my eyes locked onto it. After a few moments, the owner of that pie arose from her seat and placed it in front of me.

This act of kindness has stayed in my mind. Seventy-five years later, as we were eating at an Olive Garden restaurant, my wife, Nellie, spotted a family with a uniformed soldier. She said to me, "Let's pay for their dinner." They had already done that, but Nellie talked them into dessert. I thought this was one way I could thank that unknown German lady who gave me her pie.

A few weeks later, at another restaurant, we had a conversation with the guests at the next table. My immigration and military service were mentioned, and when we asked for the bill, the waitress told us that someone had taken care of it. A simple deed of kindness creates lasting memories – try it someday; you will like it.

Back to 1940. Military troops and police took on a notable presence, they were everywhere. If you have seen the film "*The Sound of Music*," you may remember the scenes of the song competition. In every archway was the silhouette of a policeman; it got to me. It was an indication of increased government control over our lives and reduction of freedom.

A HARBINGER OF THE AIR WAR

Defense preparations for the civilian population accelerated. Basement windows were covered with thick brick walls to protect the occupants from explosions and shrapnel. Sections of basement ceilings were reinforced with wooden beams to serve as bomb shelters. Door-sized sections of basement brick walls next to adjacent houses were reduced to half thickness so that they could easily be opened for escape routes. Each side of those walls had the required tools in place. All citizens, including children, had to participate in escape practice and fire fighting procedures,. This was serious business.

I cannot find any historical information to support the next statement, but I remember distinctly hearing about the ban on taking pets into air raid shelters. We had no neighbors with pets; therefore, I did not know this rule directly from a pet owner, but I was saddened by such low regard for family pets. I also did not know that foreign forced laborers were also banned from seeking protection in air raid shelters

At that time, we had not had any air raids. Mandatory training for air raid survival was administrated by the Party, and sometimes it had the appearance of a block party. Fire fighting equipment received special attention; on each stair landing were buckets of water, bags of sand, a shovel, and an industrial-size mop to swat fires; that was a requirement enforced through inspections, and we were trained in the proper use of those tools. In addition, all laundry tubs and similar containers in the basement had to remain filled with water so that some fire fighting would be possible even if the water mains were disabled. For realism during street demonstrations, the instructor would ignite a dreaded white phosphorous charge.

I hated the practice of donning the gas mask. The German mask was a full-faced rubber device that fitted tightly over the face, like a glove, and in the process of putting it on, it pulled the hair painfully. I never completed the task – at least not during practice.

During an air raid, everyone had to get off the street and enter the nearest shelter. To easily locate the reinforced section of a basement, each front doorway had three large white letters to indicate: “Front”, “Rear,” “Right,” “Left.” For example: “SHL” meant that the shelter is in the back of the basement on the left side. Even in 1982, some of these shelter directions were still legible on rough stucco walls.

Windows had to have internal covers to block light which could potentially attract airplanes. Every evening, the police would patrol the streets and ring doorbells and yell if any light was visible. It always bothered me when slag was dumped at the mill during the night, because the sky would light up all over the city. A tremendous effort was exerted for preparedness; however, nothing prepared us for what lay ahead – the hellish carpet bombing – nothing.

The last visible additions to the defense system were over-sized black silhouettes of a man painted on house walls, with the words:

"Psst! Feind hoert mit!" "Psst! Enemy is listening!" It is the equivalent to "Loose Lips Sink Ships."

From now on, streets were dark at night. Vehicles had small marker lights, two white ones in front and two red ones in the rear. Traffic crawled at a snail's pace. It was an eerie feeling – the constant drone of motors with no vehicles visible. It felt as if we were amid a dense, but invisible fog, with shadowy ghosts showing only pairs of red and white eyes slowly moving through the streets.

In the late thirties, Hitler had established a decree: anyone greeting a person on the street had to do so with the raised right arm Nazi salute and the word, "Heil Hitler" – everyone, including little children. On Hitler's birthday, April 20, we had to hold that arm up during the singing of the entire national anthem – too much effort for a little boy. I did not know at that time that the Nazis had special courts just to convict non-saluters.

About that degree, in retrospect, Hitler must have gotten that idea from the William Tell story, but there was a major difference between the Swiss and German versions. William Tell had a choice – he had a weapon, a crossbow and an extra arrow; we did not – we were not allowed to own weapons.

THE FIGHTING COMES HOME

The first air raid took place on a cloudless day in the summer of 1943. It was a short one, a hint of things to come. We did not expect to hear thunder, but there was what sounded like an enormous thunderclap. Word spread quickly; a bomb had fallen on a popular restaurant located three blocks from us, between the Catholic Church and the elementary school. It was a major attraction for a few days, something new and unusual. Within a short time, the government had repaired the damage.

A few weeks later came another attack. This one took down the center of a three-story apartment building on the other side of the factory, about one mile away. The scene attracted quite a crowd. The building was beyond repair. As the war progressed, the intervals between raids shortened, the severity increased, and we could remain in our own neighborhoods to see the results. The novelty was gone, and so was the ability to repair damaged buildings.

For quite a few months Air raids were relatively light, because the royal air force did not have enough planes to make our lives miserable. Apparently, my mother feared for our lives enough to have several extended stays in areas away from the industrial targets. I do not recall ever having a good explanation for our travels, but I did appreciate knowing that we did not have to get up at night and go into the bomb shelter. We stayed in several small towns, but I don't remember all of them; it was like taking several small vacations.

Once we stayed in a small farming village near Hanover, Hoehne in the Luneburger Heide, a beautiful heath country. Life there was uneventful and after three or four months we returned home. While we were there, I had noticed a few changes prompted by the war. A local saw mill had shut down because the owner's sons had been drafted into the army. One bedroom in the house where we lived was used entirely for food storage; a tall pile of dried sugar beet chips covered most of the floor. What I did not see was the Bergen-Belsen Concentration Camp, thirty miles away, where Anne Frank died a few years later.

One particularly enjoyable place to stay was in Rot am See, a large farming community near Nuernberg and Würzburg. We lived in a farm/inn that offered basic comforts. We had acres of forests and farm fields for our playgrounds; life was good and safe. For some reason, we went home for a short time, probably to check on things. Travel was still easy and safe, even in trains filled to capacity, because special compartments were reserved for "Mothers with Children," and there were no fighter planes strafing trains. When we returned, we brought along souvenirs: little steel fragments of bombs.

By this time, all my adult relatives were in the Army. Dad was a machine gunner and went to France. Uncle Karl was a Rifleman and took part in "Operation Barbarossa," the surprise attack on Russia. Uncle Bertie and Uncle Willie were mechanics in motorized units on the East Front. I never knew what Uncle Heinz did. I shudder at the thought what my uncle in the SS might have done on his March into

Russia. I knew him as a kind gentleman, but the SS wasn't known for kindness.

Sometime in early spring 1942, Uncle Kurt had joined the American army. I knew nothing about him other than he was an uncle in America. He was the last male member of our family to join the fight. He harbored a lot of anti-German sentiment that originated during the twenties. In 1957, he still blamed the Jews for Germany's financial woes and the start of the war. My two Grandfathers were spared from the military service; one of them built patterns to make guns from cast iron, the other one built rifles

The Winter of 1941 brought lots of snow that remained white for weeks. Back home the industrial pollution was so bad that the snow would turn brown in a few hours, and elementary schools closed early for the day to let children enjoy the clean snow for the short time it stayed white. Rot am See was a little paradise. Around Christmas the inn had sponsored a dance, and I saw a disturbing sight: my mother was dancing with a strange man. I got between the two in protest, because it seemed wrong to me. I also noticed that she was alive and happy as I had never seen her. Today I understand; the stranger offered respect and kindness, something her husband should have done more often.

December 31, 1941; I experienced the first episode of something that would later plague me for years: PTSD. I was asleep at midnight when explosions took place outside our window. It sounded like an air raid, and I went into a screaming spell. I experienced horrible fear. I did not know the custom of welcoming the new year with fireworks.

One day Mom came home from the post office; she was crying. She had just received a telegram with the message that her youngest brother, my Uncle Karl, had been killed in action on the Russian front. I still have the letter from his company commander in which he assured Mom that Uncle Karl had died instantly from the explosion of a mortar shell, and that he did not suffer. Uncle Karl was my favorite uncle; he was cheerful and knew how to entertain children.

The time had come to return home. Why? I don't know. This last half year had been peaceful, happy, and safe from attacks. We waited at the station for the express train. It came – packed to capacity with soldiers. The stationmaster refused to let us get on. My petite mother of ninety-eight pounds read him his rights; that train would not go without us. In the meantime, the soldiers had carried us boys and our luggage over their heads into the middle of a coach. The stationmaster relented and the soldiers offered to lift my mother into the compartment the same way we went. Soldiers were everywhere. We boys sat on their laps, and they offered this same seating arrangement for my mother; she declined. They were young and happy, joking and laughing – ready to be sacrificed.

AIR RAIDS AND INCREASING DANGER

As the train entered the Rhine Valley, I noticed destruction, especially near railroad installations. During the six-mile streetcar ride in Duisburg, we saw several destroyed houses. These were disturbing sights. Our neighborhood had some damage. During the next months, air raid warnings and air raids became weekly events. They were not severe yet, and they served as effective survival training. Every alarm was scary; we never knew where the hits would be or if it was just precautionary, because we may have been in the flight path to another city.

The drill was always the same: when the sirens went off at night, get up, take the suitcase with important documents and valuables standing next to the bed, go to the shelter area in the basement, make sure all lights are turned off, turn on the radio and wait. Listening to the radio was restricted to German stations. To listen to foreign broadcast was against the law and resulted in punishment. At times we could hear the distant drones of planes going to another city; their approach always caused anxiety. Some nights the "all clear" would sound soon after the alarm, and we would return to our bedrooms upstairs. At best, the consequences of air raid alarms were uncertain, because the Ruhr area had such a high concentration of potential targets.

The Allies used German radio frequencies during air raids to transmit depressing messages to demoralize the civilian population:

sounds of exploding bombs were followed by the sound of a collapsing building and a child's scream, “Mother!” These broadcasts were realistic, and it was not long before we heard similar sounds without the aid of a radio.

As the war progressed the air raids came more frequently, and every bedtime brought the same question, “Will they come tonight?” When they did come, the warble of the sirens was enough to boost the adrenaline flow, cause fear and anxiety, and engage the autopilot for the trip to the basement. In every aspect of our lives uncertainty ruled.

One early evening a bomber convoy passed the edge of Duisburg on the way to Oberhausen to attack a synthetic fuel plant. We watched from the basement door to the garden. Searchlights filled the sky, and tracers from “88” guns produced beautiful fireworks. Then came the moment we always feared: the lead bomber marked the target by dropping a magnesium flare.

Because of its shape we called it the “Christmas Tree.” After the tree was set, an indescribable din followed: screaming falling bombs, earth shaking explosions, and depending on the targets and the type of bombs used, an ominous red glow in the sky from fires. Every “Christmas tree,” had the same unmistakable and well heeded message: “Take cover now!” The refinery became a frequent daytime target. We always knew when the planes were en route, because many barrage balloons would appear in the sky over the target area.

Dad came home on furlough a few times, and usually we had a token air raid to harass us. During one of those small raids, Dad was going to stay upstairs. With Dad home, the tough soldier, nothing could happen to us, and by this time the raids had not been huge. I stayed with him. It did not take long to realize that the bombs were getting closer, and that Dad didn't have any way to stop them. I never again missed a trip to the shelter.

During one furlough, Dad instigated a practical joke on Mom, and it turned out to be very cruel. Mom was asleep on the sofa. Just above her head, Kurt and I banged large pot lids together, and Dad produced a powerful whistle with his mouth. It sounded just like an air raid, and Mom looked terrified when she jumped off the sofa. I regretted taking part in that joke.

During Dad's last visit home, the air raids had gotten big and nasty. The bombs fell nearby and shook the ground. Dad could not handle being defenseless, hunkering down with uncertainty about what was going on outside. He went to watch from the front door. We knew for certain what was going on: the RAF and USAF were dropping bombs on us to kill us, and the best place to be was in a protective shelter. After the war, psychologist explained that civilian population suffered worse mentally from bombing than soldiers did in battle. The difference lay in the fact that civilians were helpless victims without the means to fight back.

Gradually the Allies had amassed huge numbers of airplanes, and they also had developed a strategy that was new to warfare: carpet bombing. For the reader to better understand the reasons for those merciless attacks on civilians, I shall interrupt my story to elaborate on what historians have called, "The Greatest Crime in History."

THE ALLIES' JUSTIFICATION FOR BOMBINGS

German air defense efforts had started as early as 1933, long before the need arose, and long before massive air attacks were included in military strategic planning. Military buildup and forced annexation of parts of Europe by Germany had given strong evidence of Hitler's intention of World Domination and a way to achieve that goal, but the League of Nations did nothing to stop him.

Looking ahead toward required responses, England's Prime Minister Stanley Baldwin predicted a gruesome method to win a potential war: *[Our best defense] is in offense, which means that you have to kill more women and children more quickly than the enemy can if you want to save yourself."*

At the start of the war, the German Luftwaffe (Air Force) had attacked several English cities that resulted in major destruction and loss of civilian's lives: The *Battle of Britain.* While the initial targets were military installations, and because of navigational errors, the destruction moved to civilian targets. British Air Marshall Sir Arthur Harris had this response, "*The Nazis entered the war under the childish illusion that they were going to bomb everybody else, but nobody was going to bomb them. They sowed the wind, and now they are going to reap the whirlwind. There are a lot of people who say that bombing can never win a war. Well, my answer is, 'It has never been tried yet, and we shall see'."* Sir Arthur Harris earned the nickname "*Bomber Harris*."

He predicted thousand-bomber raids to carpet-bomb German cities as soon as the planes were available. Other than destroying the war machinery, which also included the workforce, the goal was to induce such a level of fear and panic, that the population would rise up and overthrow the Government. He achieved only the first part: fear and panic, but how can an unarmed nation of people overthrow a superbly armed and highly organized Government? Germany had the opposite of the American Second Amendment: no civilian could own a gun. I never touched a gun until 1957, after I had enlisted in the American Army.

Some historian had commented on the comparative economic difference between destroying a factory and killing a worker: a process can usually be rebuilt in a few weeks, but it takes twenty years to train a skilled worker.

By the spring of 1943, the RAF had the sufficient quantity of bombers to start the mass destruction of German cities. One of the Allied propaganda leaflets dropped over Germany pointed out that "Fortress Germany has no roof." The attacks consisted of coordinated drop sequences with specific bomb types to maximize their effectiveness: explosives to destroy streets and impair travel of rescue vehicles, and time delayed explosives to create an unexpected danger during follow-up rescue and cleanup operations. High explosive bombs were used to destroy windows and blow tile roofs apart, which was then followed by an assortment of explosives and firebombs. Without windows and roofs, the firebombs would increase their effectiveness by generating drafts in burning buildings.

To add psychological stress for the people in the targeted area, many bombs had noise generators attached. As a falling bomb increases its vertical speed, the resulting sound changes from a low-level hum to an intense high-pitched scream that reaches its peak at the moment of impact. It did not take long to recognize that moment, but it was impossible to tell if it would be on our house or in the next block; the noise was that intense.

WAR ON THE HOME FRONT

Frequency and intensity of air raids gradually increased until there was hardly a safe place in the Ruhr Valley. After my immigration to America, during conversations about the war, several people had told me, “We never bombed churches, schools, and hospitals.” Those people had no idea about the complexity of dropping a five-hundred-pound load carried by a plane flying at 200 mph at 20,000 feet onto a small target. The famous Norden Bomb Sight was supposed to enable bombardiers to “Drop a Bomb into a Pickle Barrel.” So much for theory; a hit within a mile was still considered “on target.” Neither did they know that civilian targets were not only not avoided, but they were deliberately chosen. In Allied air raid logs that can now be viewed on the Internet, a frequent target destination was “General Population.”

One of my responses was, “I agree that the Allies bombed only military targets. When bombers crossed the German border, they only had one military target: Germany.” Later during the war, the air forces, instead of aiming for target areas would specify an easily identifiable target called ‘the aiming point’. The scatter of bombs around that ‘aiming point’ was wide enough to include the intended target area. What were good aiming points? Churches; they are tall, distinctive buildings, and they are easily recognizable from a high altitude.

The Geneva Convention has strong language against taking civilian hostages, and most countries are signatories to that International Law.

When millions of German civilians in their own country were being attacked from the air, were they considered hostages and targets? Apparently not, Sir Harris did not consider civilians targets; Germans had become hostages by their own government.

A few times people have asked me if I was in the war, and my usual response was, "I was too young to be a soldier, but I had been a designated target."

PROPAGANDA BRAIN WASHING MISINFORMATION

I was too young to understand the concepts of propaganda, brainwashing, and misinformation, but I saw the effects, and I was a victim. Throughout the war I was told about the victorious German Army that destroyed the uncivilized hordes that caused of all our problems. Weekly newsreels showed the Blitz Krieg (Lightning War) as defensive actions to free Germany from its oppressors and safeguard the future of the superior German race. We were the good people.

At first these victories and tales of military superiority sounded convincing, but later in the war, after the cities were turned to dust, we secretly questioned the official stories. There was evidence to the contrary all around us, but openly discussing those discrepancies could have been a death sentence for the messenger.

There were occasional displays of military armament. A sobering one was the assortment of Allied aerial bombs that had been recovered and defused. More cheerful was the appearance of a German light armored reconnaissance vehicle. It stood on the broad sidewalk in a main shopping area. We were allowed to look inside and talk to the crew. Ten years later, I mentioned the event at work. One of the journey men knew what I was talking about; he had been one of the crew members.

Eastern European nationals and Jews were openly reviled. I was unaware of what Jews were; they were negatively depicted, especially in children's stories: a group of unshaven men with huge hooked noses and in tattered clothing would be shown in some disorderly activity, while on the next page a platoon of handsome German soldiers was sitting in precise order riding in a truck.

One time during our temporary stay in a small town, my brother and I were walking on the Main Street past a farm. A rough looking farmhand stood there, and I asked him, "Are you German or Pollock?" He did not say a word and walked up to me; he smacked my face with a powerful blow of his hand. Obviously, he was German. I never again questioned anyone's nationality. This time the racial profiler was the victim.

The Evening News always had a special ending. It started with a rousing melody composed by the censored non-German composer Franz Liszt: Les Preludes. Then the announcer would discuss the victorious attacks by German submarines on Allied convoys and the tonnage sunk at sea.

Fifty years later as I watched the movie *Das boot,* I had a sudden reminder of those newscasts: the officers in the submarine had finished a meal and were listening to music from a German radio station. Suddenly, Les Preludes came on and the chief, visibly disturbed, yelled at the radio operator, "Turn it off!" The American viewer would have missed the point, but I knew at once the reason for that order: the U-boat reports were full of lies. The propaganda ministry over-inflated the numbers even when the U boats were on the defensive. Since 2019, *Les Preludes* is one of my favorite melodies, although the crescendo still produces the urge to cry – the memories are that strong.

What the propaganda ministry could not hide was the increasing destruction of cities and railroads. I could not understand why the world around me was crumbling while we were winning the war. Even in late 1944, when the Allied troops were poised twenty miles from us to cross the Rhine, the last natural defensive line in Germany, we were told of wonder weapons that would destroy the invaders and assure swift victory. That did not make sense even to an eight-year-old, but mention it openly and it becomes treason.

Around that time, I saw the contrail of a V-2 rocket streaking west through the sky. I ran excitedly into the basement and hollered, "I saw a V-2!" Everyone raised a finger across the lips and said, "Shh! Be Quiet!"

Both sets of my grandparents lived in Essen, the home of Krupp, Germany's armament manufacturing giant. Several times Mom took me to her parents' home to stay for the weekend. My brother may have been at a boy's camp at those times. We had a few nearby air raids; their house did not have a basement; it was scary.

On one of those visits we went to a Department store three or four blocks away. It was an interesting place and I had wandered off. When

I realized my mistake, my grandparents were gone. They could not find me and went home without me. I had been abandoned. I went outside and walked in the direction to where I thought we had come from. I was lucky and found our house which looked like a hundred other row houses in that neighborhood. It is bad enough to be abandoned, but during this unsafe time the feeling turned into panic. What had my grandparents been thinking?

Normally the school year started in the Spring, but times were not normal, and I had entered the first grade in the Fall of 1942. Schools had no shelters to protect hundreds of children; therefore, when the early warning system detected a probable attack on Duisburg, kids were sent home. There was always ample time to walk the three blocks home. We came home one day when we had a small raid – no one was there. Our neighbors had gone out, and my mother was at work. My brother and I were alone in the basement. It was quite scary, but fortunately, the short raid had been targeted a few blocks away.

A few weeks earlier my mother had passed the police station. A window opened, and a voice commanded her to come inside. "You are going to work in the factory." She protested and said that she could not leave her two children alone at home. "We all have children," was the reply, and she received a stern lecture about patriotism and the need for all people to contribute to the victory. She did her duty, and we had a few more occasions to go to the empty house after an alarm was sounded.

Air raids became more frequent and got more intense. "The Battle of the Ruhr" had begun, and we received the first of the big raids promised by "Bomber Harris." During the night of May 12, 1943, 577 British bombers attacked downtown, the ancient part of the city. They dropped 1,055 explosive bombs, 106 blockbusters, and 128,000 firebombs. 272 people perished, and of those, 233 died inside bomb shelters. Over 96,000 people became homeless during this raid.

I was lucky, for we lived about four miles from the inferno, at the edge of the prime target, but the noise and the red glow in the sky left a lasting impression. The anti-aircraft guns were positioned throughout town and they added considerably to the din.

CHILDREN'S EVACUATION TO SAFETY

Because of this devastating raid, a program was introduced to remove children from cities subjected to massive raids. The term "evacuation" was avoided; instead it was called: Erweiterte Kinder Landverschickung," which translates into "Expanded Children's Excursions" and did not emphasize the escape from danger. The move became mandatory.

There were two groups of evacuees: pregnant women and mothers with very young children, and children between ages six and ten. The latter would be sent either to evacuation camps or to foster homes. Foster parents received extra food rations and two marks per child per day. An estimated three million children were taken out of cities and sent to safe locations in towns out of reach of the Allied bombers, and I was one of them.

Shortly after the devastating raid in May, Mom took us and two small suitcases to the main railroad station. We boarded a long train packed with children. To where? No one said.

The trip was slow. Several times our train waited at a siding for a long time until a military transport passed and allowed our low priority train to continue. The scenery of Southern Germany is beautiful and the cities we passed through had not yet been damaged by bombing. I don't recall if we slept twice on the train or just once. To get ready for the night we would take on an upright position in our seats and then lean to one side to semi recline sideways. By morning there was no resemblance of that orderly arrangement.

A highlight of any train trip to the South always was the bridge at Remagen, seventy miles from home. Just before the train crossed the bridge, it traveled through a three-quarter-mile-long tunnel. There were no lights, and the chugging of the steam engine was quite loud. Then suddenly the train left the tunnel and entered the bridge over the beautiful Rhine River. It got quiet. The scenery on that stretch of the Rhine is gorgeous. We were out of the Ruhr district, and I felt safe. The last member of our family to cross the Remagen Bridge was Uncle Kurt, Dad's brother. He did it with General Patton’s Third Army.

LIFE IN FOSTER CARE

We did not know where we were going. The trip ended around midnight in a beautiful train station. We were in Vienna, Austria, six hundred miles from home. We walked to a large auditorium that was filled with cots and got a night of real sleep. The next morning we traveled in small groups on regularly scheduled trains. After about two hours, we arrived at the small town of Neudoerfl, near the old Austro-Hungarian border, and my brother and I were taken to our foster homes.

The Marchard's were my foster parents; they had one daughter, Louise; we were both seven years old. My brother lived with the Pfister's next door. The row house was divided into fifteen compact two room units with three apartments sharing a main entrance. The town and surrounding area were beautiful and quiet. We were far away from the war and physically safe.

Kurt's family was a bundle of fun. I could hear their laughter and see evidence of happiness, but I was not allowed to visit them. Our doors were only inches apart, but I was not allowed to enter. Mr. Marchard worked as an attendant in a mental hospital. Mrs. Marchard stayed at home. Her brother had recently been killed in action, and, as part of the mourning process, we were not allowed to joke, laugh, or listen to the radio.

I did not know her brother's name. It was always, “My brother the Captain; he fell for the Fatherland.” I felt imprisoned. I never saw the Marchard adults smile. On one occasion, they accused me of having said bad things about the family. They interrogated me and made my life miserable. I had no one to turn to for help.

One little incident around that time influenced my behavior half a century later. In the 1990’s I did some work in the home of a family of second-generation Greek Americans, George and Bess Fotos in Huntington, WV. Bess was an excellent cook, and I ate several of her Greek meals and quite a few snacks. One day Bess asked me, “Klaus, you never turn down a meal, do you?” I replied, “No, and I don't do it for a very good reason.” I then explained what happened to me in 1943 when I lived in foster care in Austria.

A sympathetic neighbor had asked me, “Klaus, can I fix you a sandwich?” My self-esteem was near zero, I felt insecure about everything. I did not want to be a burden to anyone, and I thought the polite answer should be, “No, thank you.” The man asked again, and I gave the same answer. I was hungry and I had the full intention to say “yes” when he asked again. A half-century later, he still has not asked. My theory now is: if you do not want me to have anything don't ask, and if you ask, I assume you are sincere, and my answer will always be “yes”.

A visit to the Marchard’s relatives in a nearby town was a delight. There was a boy my age. His Dad took us to a nearby park where we ran around, played games, and had great fun. At their home we climbed up a cherry tree and picked ripe cherries. What raised my spirits the most was the fact that the Dad treated me as if I were his son. Love and respect were evident, and for a few hours I was not just a foster child kept for a fee.

Our Mother came to visit us one time, and she and I stayed in the hotel. That night I wet the bed, and I received a verbal thrashing over it. I was a mental wreck, and I had no idea that the accident was a result of my mental state. When I needed help, I got rejection.

There was however one wonderful day with the Marchard's. They were Catholic, and their daughter was to be confirmed into the church. We went to Vienna to the St. Stephen Cathedral for the ceremony. It is a huge and magnificent building. Several services were held simultaneously, and in one end was a monk's choir singing. Later, we went to the most fabulous entertainment park I had ever seen called "The Prater". It had fantastic rides, beautiful displays, and an enormous ferris wheel from which we had a great view of a beautiful undamaged city. That day was the most exciting experience I had in a very long time. A few years ago, I had purchased a tape of the movie, *"The Third Man;"* it contained scenes from that park. Oh, what memories!

On the way to Vienna I saw something that looked odd, but I was too young to put my finger on it. On the train was a man in his mid-twenties; he played an accordion to entertain passengers and collected donations. He looked perfectly healthy. Panhandlers and vagrants did not fare well in Germany under Hitler. Had he been an Entertainer to be part of the Vienna scene to uplift the spirits of passengers, he would have worn traditional regional attire. What was he doing there? Young, healthy men in their twenties were in the Army. In retrospect, he was probably an informer in disguise, a GESTAPO agent keeping watch on travelers.

We had left Vienna late that day, and the nearest train station we could reach was Wiener Neustadt, an hour's walk from home. We passed through a small village that had one streetlight in the center of town; it was a cheerful site.

For many years, I kept wondering what had been so unusual about Vienna in 1943. I had thought about that night many times. The night of our arrival felt as if I was entering a little Heaven; it was that beautiful. I realized the answer in 1968, twenty-five years later: Vienna's streets were brightly lit, the buildings had cheerful colors, and they were clean. I had never seen such a beautiful city and certainly none at night and not blacked out.

THE AIR WAR EXPANDS

One late summer day, there was an enormous air raid a few miles from us. The Allies had bombed an airfield and an airplane factory. They were able to do that after they had established air bases in the Mediterranean, and our town was no longer in a safe area. Within a few days, we gathered our belongings and we were transferred to another town. We wore yellow tags from our necks with all important data on display just like address labels on packages. Those labels included our names, ages, hometown, destination and the responsible person to notify upon arrival. Special compartments were reserved for solo-traveling children, and at every stop someone checked to assure proper delivery. The system was well organized just like UPS, except we did not have UPC codes on us.

The trip was short, about sixty miles and no more than three hours. We arrived in Ulmerfeld just before sunset. There were several families waiting to pick up their new foster children. My brother had found a family and went to his new home, leaving three other children and me. The party officials loaded us into a two-wheeled horse-drawn wagon and visited several farms in the area. I felt like excess merchandise offered for sale to the lowest bidder. About two hours after dark, a farmer's family agreed to take me in; I was the last one.

On the farm were two boys around my age, their parents, and a grandmother. Hardly a word was said; it was not a friendly welcome.

They probably did not want me and were coerced into taking me in. The boys and I got along fine; the adults tolerated me. The surrounding fields and woods made great playgrounds, and those activities made life bearable. Inside the house life was somber, and at the supper table hardly a word was spoken.

During the week, supper usually consisted of a thick slice of rye bread, some butter, a slab of cheese, and chunk of fatback. At the table were two parents, the grandmother, three boys, and two farm hands, forced laborers from a foreign country. For drinks we had a large pitcher of apple cider, but no glasses. To drink, one would take the pitcher, ceremonially wipe a small part of the rim with two fingers, then take a sip from that spot. It was then passed it on to the next person.

Slices of fatback were commonly used to make sandwiches. At one of our visits to a farm, I don't remember where, the hostess prepared such a sandwich for me. To my dismay, it included quite a few white maggots. I got a maggot-free sandwich after the lady removed the maggots and returned the same sandwich to me. Nothing was wasted.

During the Fall harvest I witnessed a scary scene. Work had lasted longer than usual; that is the nature of farming. Supper was served late, and the two laborers did not return to their camp at curfew time. Two camp officials came to the house while we were in the middle of supper. An argument between the farmer and the officials ensued. The farmer defended the laborers and their right to supper. The argument got heated, and suddenly the farmer pulled a knife from his pocket and opened a blade. I left the room in fear. To my knowledge there were no repercussions, but it was a scary situation.

The farm had an elaborate fenced-in garden. I could watch the beautiful berry bushes and red tomatoes, but I was not allowed to go inside. However, one day when everyone had gone to attend a funeral, I disobeyed that order. I had a wonderful time sampling several varieties of berries and eating fully ripened tomatoes.

The area experienced no air raids, because there was nothing of military importance. Winter came, and with it came deep snow and low temperatures. School was half an hour away – a walk on top of a ridge. A few times I made the longer trip through the valley, because on windy days the regular route was too uncomfortable. School was tolerable, but I was an outsider, and my Ruhr dialect made that obvious.

On December 6, 1943, Saint Nicholas Day, I had an experience that no adult should allow to happen. The event is an old tradition celebrated in several European countries. Saint Nicholas was born in the Third Century AD. He was a benefactor to the poor. On his visits he is accompanied by Ruprecht who wields a switch and threatens punishment for bad deeds, but Saint Nicholas intervenes and hands out small bags with gifts for the children.

Times were bad and there was not much to give, usually some nuts, fruits, cookies, etc. The two brothers received bags almost quart-sized –

mine was barely half that size. What did that say? “You are unequal, and we don't like you as much our own children.” It hurt.

During this time of separation, I always worried about the other family members. Our family of four lived in four places. Dad was stationed at Vierville-sur-mer near Caen in the Normandy area of France. Not much was happening there, and he did not get involved in fighting. Mom was at home in the middle of a primary target for the Air Forces. We heard news on the radio about the attacks and never knew if she was safe until after we received a letter from her. My brother lived about two miles from me, and, while we were physically safe, the emotional strain was heavy. Mom lived in the most dangerous location making the chance to become an orphan real.

Mother became aware of my plight through communication with my brother's foster mother. Just before Christmas, she came to take me home. We went home without Kurt; he was in a good home and had no reason to leave. The train trip through Austria and Bavaria during the Winter was a beautiful experience. We occupied a compartment reserved for mothers with children. The snow-covered land was a delight to see; it was undisturbed and peaceful.

When we arrived in Würzburg, we had to leave the train to go into an air raid shelter to sit out an air raid. There was nearby rumbling, but the attack missed the train station. The atmosphere in the shelter was one of apprehension: several rooms filled with strangers – few subdued conversations – people just looking at each other with blank expressions.

Then three men entered; one was wearing a military police uniform. He wore the Special Police identification: a silver crescent hanging on his chest by a chain that earned them the nickname "Chain Dogs." They had great authority. The other two men wore plain clothes. The three walked through the entire room and looked at every occupant They took one away. Who knows why? Was he an escaped prisoner, spy, or criminal?

Even as a child I sensed the oppressive nature of their behavior. During a stop-over at a railroad station, the steam engine released a safety valve – too much pressure. One of the chain dogs just about verbally ripped the driver's head off. Blowing off excess steam meant wasting precious energy needed for the Victory.

During the war years I witnessed many incidents of authoritative behavior by uniformed people. I had developed a fear of anyone in uniform or with authority; it stayed with me for a long time. After the war I had learned to ride the bicycle and I ventured out into all directions. One path would have taken me through a very busy intersection called Pollman corner. I avoided it, because in the center of the crossing stood a policeman to direct traffic, and I was sure he would stop me and give me a ticket for some minor traffic rule infraction. It took weeks before I had the courage to pass him, and when I did, he didn't pay any attention to me.

Fast forward to 1960, I was stationed at Fort Huachuca, Arizona. One late evening I drove one of my buddies to Benson to catch a bus. On the way back, a Highway Patrol car with a flashing red light appeared behind me. Panic struck. I wondered what I did wrong. The officer was very polite and checked the registration affixed to the steering column, and he asked to see my driver's license. Because of my heavy accent, he inquired about my nationality, and we had a delightful conversation; he wanted to know more about Germany. My fear had been total unwarranted, but my instinct was still fifteen years behind the time.

After we crossed the Rhine River at Remagen, increased evidence of bombardments appeared. It was not bad yet, but it was obvious that the Allies had started to wear down the system. Duisburg had received several attacks, one just before our arrival. During our streetcar ride, we saw several burning buildings and the fire trucks trying to extinguish the blazes. We stayed home until after Christmas. We had a few alarms, but nothing was serious. I received one Christmas gift: a simple wooden scooter. The first time I stepped on it fell apart. Civilian goods were not constructed well; they just did not help win the war.

A HAPPY FOSTER HOME

Mother had found a new foster home for me. Rosa, Kurt's foster mother, had a sister, Hilda, in Amstetten, five miles from Ulmerfeld, my brother's home. I was warmly received, and that warmth never left. When we got there, the government had just designated a special ration stamp to purchase blankets. We went shopping, and Mom let us pick the colors; mine was blue, and Kurt's was bright red. These blankets were valuable assets, and they served us into the early fifties, when Mom had converted mine into an overcoat. Several times the thick hem got caught between the spokes and rear fork of my bicycle and acted like an emergency brake. The coat was not suitable for bike riding, but it was warm and the only one I owned.

Hilda had a happy home, and she treated me well. I don't know if she was married. There was no man in the picture, and in Kurt's home was only a middle-aged man with a peg leg. By this time in the war, most men had become soldiers. Kurt and I could visit each other frequently. Train rides between our towns cost the equivalent of a dime. The winter was cold and long, but when spring came it was playtime. Our short street had about a dozen kids to play with. Those were happy days, except for the uncertainty about the safety of our parents.

The only problem was school, and again, I was the outsider, bullied and ridiculed. Once I had to attend special classes for kids that had been accused of having tortured animals, something I have never done.

It was very depressing for me, and my grades were poor. I knew that I could not have advanced to the next level, but that did not matter. Before I entered school after the war, my mother threw away all the documents, and there was no way to get copies. Having lost documents was common after the war and was readily accepted and a convenient excuse.

In the spring of 1944, Dad and Mom had come to visit us for a few days. We made a one-day excursion by train to a popular tourist town; I think it was Graz. I remember the wonderful time we had as a family. Another day, Dad, Kurt and I went into the forest. We ran around, slid down hills, laughed, and did what families do just for fun.

Dad was in uniform and had to stay clean. He was a good-looking soldier – a handsome man. During the excitement he lost a beautiful mechanical silver pencil with four colored inserts. We searched without success. That loss was well worth the good times we had, and for the rest of our lives we talked about the happy day when he lost the four-colored pencil; it was never forgotten.

MY LAST SIX MONTHS IN AUSTRIA

The war came closer again. Once a long train passed on the main line, and shortly thereafter, I heard airplanes and gunfire. The next day the train was pulled back into the station; it had been shot up, including the coaches with the big red crosses. It was a sad sight. All trains had a special car with anti-aircraft guns on it, usually a flatbed in the rear, but their effectiveness against several attacking planes was limited.

During one of my visits to Kurt, I misbehaved. I needed to get a 'groschen', a German dime, from Kurt to buy the return train ticket. Rosa forbade him to give it to me; I had no choice but to walk the five miles home through open country. That was a lot to ask of a seven-year-old boy. I walked. A short distance from town the police had blocked a side road. I saw the outline of a crashed Allied plane in the distance. I just kept walking.

A man on a bicycle came from the opposite direction. "Where are you going?" he asked. "To Amstetten," I answered. His reply was sadistic and caused me great anxiety, "Amstetten just had a huge air raid and most of the town is destroyed." I kept walking, and when I got to Amstetten, everything looked normal. Why would anyone tell such a lie?

One pleasant memory was the arrival of the circus. It provided a much-needed diversion from all the negative events in my life. The erection of the big tent looked like a well-rehearsed ballet. While the work was very difficult physically, the synchronized movements of the workers made it look easy. The high point of the circus was the band, the musicians wore beautiful uniforms and they produced impressive sounds.

To me, music has been and still is, a source of comfort, memories, and healing. Some of it still causes tears to flow, because the melodies bring back memories and visions of important events of my past.

Music is a universal language, and if people of all countries would make music together, even though they cannot understand a word the others speak, we would have made a serious attempt to create harmony and peace. That is my opinion. The only time I ever disliked any musical instrument was for a few years after the war. The sound of violins reminded me of the screaming bombs falling on us. I hated violins. I hated them with a passion; they caused emotional pain.

Unfortunately, my exposure to music was limited to German music. Music by foreign composers was banned. I did not hear music by Gershwin until years after the war. When I heard music from *My Fair Lady* in 1963, I was elated by the words of "G*et Me to Church on Time*." Even my Dad told me, "American musicals – that is not music. Wagner, Beethoven, and Strauss – that is real music." Well, so much for brain washing.

The Allies, too, did ban music at the end of the war – the German National Anthem. The text contained nothing to further the Nazi ideas, but, after you lose a war, you do, or don't do, what the victors demand. The beauty of that song is the melody composed in 1797 by Joseph Haydn.

A carnival came to town, something like America's County Fair. I mostly looked at the rides, because I had very little money. Then a nice man invited me to ride with him in the dodgem car. It was fun, and he kept giving me free rides. Suddenly, several adults came to us and ran him off. I didn't know why, and I was unhappy. Many years later, I realized the danger I had been in; the man was probably a pervert. I was fortunate those people had protected me.

One of my favorite rides to watch was the merry go round with the colorful horses gracefully galloping in circles, and in the center was a calliope. I was fascinated by the animated instruments. This mechanical music machine looked and sounded beautiful, and that was what I needed. I had seen and heard too much ugly stuff. This was an escape into a different World – a peaceful World that made me happy.

At school we had been given collection cans, bright red with swastikas and with seals at the openings. My job was to walk the streets and ask for donations for homeless children or something like that. I was shy and insecure, and I silently held up the can and hoped people would put a little money into the slot. The real purpose for the collections was to raise money to help finance the war, but I did not find out about it until many years later.

We had a few small air raids nearby. I think they were intended to harass the population more than to destroy industry, but they were a sign that the war situation was getting worse. One night, we heard a bombing raid maybe ten miles away. I saw two falling, spinning fireballs. A bomber had been hit and broken into two pieces. I felt sad. Yes, these were enemy planes, but there were people in them, engulfed in fire and falling to their deaths. This scene stuck with me a long time. The propaganda ministry depicted Americans as primitive people, capable only of evil deeds, but I felt compassion for them.

In 2012, I worked in a house near my home. "My husband was in Germany during the war." "How were you there?" "Air Force." "What did you fly in?" "Fortress." "Did you know Duisburg?" "Yes." "What crew position did you hold?" "Bombardier." His answers were terse. The ninety-two-year-old had difficulty holding back tears – he had compassion for the people of his targets, and probably, for the first time he talked to one of his victims. I told him that I had no more feelings of animosity toward the fliers, because I now understood that the bombings were not their decisions. After his death, his widow told me that he understood my sentiment. I hope that I had eased the burden on his conscience.

In the sixties, I had befriended an immigrant from a Middle Eastern country. He had served in the German Army. He told me about a devastating attack on Würzburg . The Allies had dropped leaflets telling the citizens to leave town because of the planned attack. The government prevented the evacuation, and he watched from a distance as the town was pulverized. He cried.

June 6, 1944 passed without fanfare: D-day. We were not told details about the battle, because it obviously was a defeat, but, according to newsreels, Germany was still winning the war. We were always defending the Fatherland against these terrible intruders. "Untermenschen," sub-humans that were inferior to the pure German race. A short time later, came a letter from Mom, "Dad is missing in action." He had been at the center of the invasion on Omaha Beach. What else could happen to make my life miserable and hopeless?

Many times, during school vacations and on weekends when I had nothing to do, I'd walk downtown just to look at the city and the train traffic. A small restaurant on the way offered a tasty soft drink for a groschen. Older people in America recall it as "phosphate;" It was water with fruit juice for flavoring and a squirt of phosphate to give it that tart, tingly taste. It has been replaced by bottled sodas.

On one of my walks downtown I went into the railroad station. Most stations have a nice restaurant and a bar, because trains are the main transportation, and travelers need to eat, but most importantly, drink beer. Two men sat at the end of the bar, and a woman was the server. I walked up to the bar looked straight up, and with confidence I told the waitress, "I want a beer." I don't know why I did it.

She turned to the row of taps, took a pint-sized glass, and started filling it. The process takes several minutes, because the law is specific about filling the glass and removing excess foam. She gave me the glass and I gave her a groschen. The two men paid no attention to me. I had the beer. Now what? I really did not like beer, but I had to keep face. I drank half of the pint. I was eight years old.

In contrast, at the train station in Rot am See was a candy vending machine with a warning label, “Children under fourteen are forbidden to use it.” But there wasn’t any problem for a child to buy beer in a store and carry it home to his parents. Beer does not carry the stigma it does in America. It is a beverage, and it's a good one.

Twenty years ago, my friend offered a perfectly logical reason for serving me the beer: “The Americans are coming from the West, the Russians are coming from the East, the Air Forces are coming from above; who knows how much longer the boy is going to live. Let him have a beer; it may be the last thing he has to enjoy before he gets killed.”

I stopped at the cobbler to pick up my only pair of shoes, and I told him that I was going back home. We said our goodbyes and I left. He came after me and gave me something I had never seen: it was red, juicy, and tasted sweet: watermelon. There were a few other foods I had never seen: bananas, oranges, and lemons, and it would be years before they became available. I don't remember if Kurt and I traveled home un-escorted, as was a common way for children to travel during the war. Our city did not look as it did when we left it a year before, and we had no clue that even greater changes would take place during the next few months.

THE BEGINNING OF THE END

Duisburg had taken on a different look. Well-known landmarks no longer looked familiar, especially downtown. Our favorite eating place, Cafe Wilms, was now a burned-out shell among a block of ruins. In the suburbs there was major destruction, but it did not look as bad as downtown. This city is relatively narrow and long, and it contains several open spaces and factories between populated centers. This geography resulted in an abnormally high number of "misses" during the Allied bombing.

Another miss factor was the high level of industrial pollution that created a dense layer of smog over the city and made it difficult to identify the targets. Not far from home, we passed two buildings constructed with metal shells: the steel houses. To me, they represented the ultimate safety; steel houses can't burn, was my reasoning. I envied their owners for years.

My neighborhood had taken quite a few hits, but it was nothing like the city center. Schools were closed now. Closed schools made male teachers available for military service and women for work in factories. Life had become dangerous everywhere because of the Allied air superiority.

To provide safe shelters during air raids, the city had constructed several high-rise bunkers. One of these was located just around the corner from our house. The building rises eight stories above ground and several more below. Extremely thick concrete walls and upper ceiling were supposed to repel any bomb. We had taken a tour of the bunker to get acquainted with it and to receive space assignments. There were lots of narrow corridors connecting the small rooms. It was a depressing sight. We decided there was too great a chance to get trapped inside, and we did not register for occupancy; we preferred the familiarity of our fortified basement shelter.

Across the street from the bunker was a large one floor underground shelter. It was some kind of civic office. We went inside it one day; I don't know why. When a uniformed Nazi official walked by, my brother did not salute him, and he received a verbal thrashing. Mom stood up for Kurt; that resulted in an argument with raised voices. Such incidents always scared me, because I was aware of the power the uniformed officers had over us.

A new slogan had appeared in our daily life, "Men between sixteen and sixty belong to the front." I remember vividly hearing it. Our neighbor's son, Herman, had his apprenticeship shortened by one year, almost one-third, so that he was available for the army. Germany was running out of men.

Air raids became more frequent and intense. We now had several daily warnings, because so many targets were in close proximity that the intended ones were difficult to predict. A new system of alarms was introduced. The old one had two signals: "alarm" and "all clear." The new one added an "advance warning," which meant that Allied planes were on their way to our general area. Then the regular alarm would be sounded when the probability of an attack was high. When the target was identified as our town the "acute alarm" was given.

Evenings were always full of apprehension – waiting for the next raid. After supper, Mom had cleared the table and washed the dishes. She would sit at the kitchen table, knit, read a book, and listen to the radio – all at the same time. Knitting was something many women had done right after the war with Russia had started; they knitted mittens for our soldiers on the Eastern Front, because the German army had been ill prepared for the harsh Russian winter. We called them "shooting gloves" because they separated the thumb and index finger from the other three to minimize heat loss.

By this time, knitting was routine homework to keep up with the clothing needs of two growing boys and the unavailability of clothing. Mom had become an expert of salvaging garments, socks, sweaters, and gloves, and converting them to similar items of bigger sizes. Her skills kept us dressed into the early fifties

The radio had become the early warning system and gave us important information. When we boys got too wild, Mom would ask us to simmer down so she could listen to the radio. We got wild again, this time Mom turned around and gave us a stern look without saying a word. We knew what that meant. The third time we got noisy she would jump out of the chair, grab a coat hanger or a ladle, or any item to extend the reach of her hand, and then she gave us the well-deserved spanking. "Third strike out" was my unwitting introduction to a baseball rule.

I did not know for sixty years why the air forces were so busy in our area around that time. In March, during "Operation Plunder," the Allies tried to cross the Rhine at Wesel, twenty miles from us. In May, the Allies had tried to cross the Rhine River at Arnhem, not too far from us, during "Operation Market Garden." Not once was anything said to indicate the location of the Allies, and we had no idea that we were almost in shouting distance from them. The skies were extremely busy during those months.

During one raid, bombs hit nearby, and we had several broken windows and fallen plaster. A lady came to help with the clean-up. Her name was Wanda; I noticed nothing unusual about her. Mom treated her well, and she was good with us kids. She looked like any ordinary woman. She was a Ukrainian forced laborer – a modern slave.

Around the same time, Mom had sent me to the store to buy a pie crust. It looked good and I was hungry. I was always hungry. I took a small bite out of the raised border. The resulting gap did not look right. If I take small uniform bites around the crust, I thought, it will look like a scalloped edge produced at the bakery. I was wrong. The resulting whipping from Mom was not considered child abuse.

There were a few more events centered around food. Mom had found extra butter and sugar, and she baked a large sheet cake. To make it especially good, she added extra sugar and quite a few lumps of butter all over it. After the cake had cooled, the only way we could cut it was with a knife hit hard with a hammer. The melted butter had combined with the sugar and produced a type of brittle.

Another time, Mom had baked a beautiful chocolate cake with fantastic icing. We had a lady visitor in the living room and Mom ask Kurt to get the cake from the kitchen. Kurt saw a chance to emulate our Dad. He carried the cake on one hand and above his shoulders, stumbled, and fell flat on his face. The cake entered the living room before he did. I benefited from the accident by having a lot of mis-shaped cake to eat.

After hearing so many daily alarm sequences, we began to ignore some of them. One day, my brother was at the grocery store around the corner. The sequence started, and Mom asked me to call Kurt home to the shelter. I found him in a long grocery line. He would not go home with me. "I have been in this line a long time, and I don't want to lose my place," because we already experienced a considerable food shortages.

By this time, we had received news from Dad; he was in a military hospital in an area like Appalachia. He was recuperating and far away from the fighting.

On June 6th, D-Day, during a hasty retreat at Omaha Beach, he had tripped a German antipersonnel mine, a "Bouncing Betty." The explosion destroyed his left foot. Army medics carried him to safety behind German lines, and after two amputations necessitated by gangrene, he was transported to a regular hospital deep inside Germany. This terrible injury most probably saved his life by removing him from the front line.

REIGN OF TERROR

October 14, 1944, was the worst day of my entire life. Several times, I was certain that I would be killed by a powerful explosion or left to slowly die, buried under the collapsed house. In the morning the alarm sounded, and we went down to the shelter, turned on the radio and waited. The next step in the alarm sequence sounded: a large group of bombers was passing over Venlo at the Dutch border, and it was approaching Duisburg. Within a few minutes, we heard the drone of the airplane engines, lots of them, more than ever before, and the acute warning sounded.

The radio announcer said, "Acute danger for Duisburg," but we already knew that, because we heard the drone of the airplane engines, and before she could finish the sentence, we heard and felt a powerful explosion, and the power went off. For the next hour or two we were pounded by countless bombs. I don't recall the actual duration of the attack; how do you define "Eternity?"

It was horrible! The bombs kept falling with their characteristic screams, and when they hit Mom would throw herself over us to protect us with her body, over and over again. The concussions of the blasts shook us and made the candles flicker. We heard several buildings in the neighborhood collapse.

When there was a lull in falling bombs, the noise was dominated by the firing of the powerful eighty-eight-millimeter guns. They were all over town, and the nearest one was only two blocks from the house. The din was unreal.

Although the planes traveled four or five miles above us, their combined engine noise was quite loud. When many planes travel in close proximity, an acoustical phenomenon occurs: the beat frequency. It is a rhythmic peaking of engine sounds produced when many sounds reach their peak at the same time. This combined sound is louder than the sum of all sounds. It was evidence that there are many planes. “Whooo, Whooo, Whooo.” It was an ominous sign about what was above us.

The intensity and frequency of the explosions turned seconds into minutes – minutes into hours – an hour into eternity. The raids were more than physical destruction of our town – they destroyed our sanity.

Finally, after two hours, or an eternity, I am not sure which it was, the explosions stopped, the sky got quiet, the eighty-eight gun fire stopped, and the “all clear” was assumed, because without electricity, the sirens could not wail and give the official notice. We went up to survey the damage. Doors were ripped off their jambs, windows broken, plaster and glass slivers everywhere and furniture tossed throughout the rooms. The apartment was no longer fit to be occupied.

The outside looked bad, too: craters in the streets, collapsed and burning houses. Three houses from us, the top floor of a three-story house was on fire. The occupants carried many valuables and furniture onto the street to save them. They watched as the fire worked its way to the bottom of the house – floor by floor; it was a race against time. The white phosphorus won, because there was nothing to stop it. There were too few fire engines, too many fires, and not enough water to put out the blazes.

Kurt and I walked several blocks from our house; the picture was the same everywhere. In a few hours our World had been drastically changed, but we did not know this transformation was not yet completed. Electricity, gas, and water were cut off. People everywhere were frantically trying to rescue their belongings. Our neighborhood did not look like it did this morning.

We spent some time clearing the floor of debris and valuables, putting furniture back into place, and deciding if we could make the apartment livable. It became clear that from now on our new apartment would have to be the air raid shelter in the basement. Upstairs was history. After this big raid, we spent most of the daytime with neighbors in their first floor living room, because there was less damage than upstairs, and the trip to the shelter was shorter.

I don't recall what we did for supper. Cooking was out of the question. In disastrous times like this, people adapt and make do with what is available. We adapted; we were lucky to be alive. Evening came, and we settled down for the night. Herman, the neighbor's eighteen-year-old son, a soldier in a tank, was home on furlough; three adults, a teenager, and two children waiting for the next attack. It came around midnight. Without electricity, we had no warning from the radio, and the alarm sirens were silent, but we heard the ominous sound of approaching airplanes: "Whoo, Whoo, Whooo." Again, we were pounded with bombs.

The screaming bombs came in waves and seemed far away and next to us – everywhere. It is difficult enough for a child to understand death at some undetermined future date, but to face the possibility in the next few seconds and many times is mental torture. My biggest fear was becoming buried alive under our collapsed house. That night, I experienced several hours of potential life-ending threats. The uncertainty of what was going to happen to us, with the added realization that more of it was coming our way, was enough to induce a bit of insanity. Our nerves were raw.

Then it happened – a loud impact noise – the house shook as if it was in agony. Mom covered us again with her body. Was this the end? We looked at the ceiling expecting it to come down on us. It would take a few agonizing seconds to find out, but again, it didn't.

The three adults and the teenager raced upstairs. Kurt and I were left alone. Panic struck, but the earlier frequent training guided us almost automatically; we moved into the hallway of the basement where the walls were close together, the ceiling is the strongest, and where the thin escape wall was located. The adults did not have to tell us; our reaction to the situation was a learned habit. The stairs where a few feet from us around the corner.

The racket outside was horrible, and suddenly, a huge blast ripped the heavy oak front door off its hinges; it flew into the basement and crashed with a loud thunder against a wall next to us. A *"Block Buster"* had exploded nearby. With the door open, the noise level increased, and we could hear a new sound: the staccato of incendiary bombs crashing onto the pavement. Would it ever end? Kurt wept openly – I was too stunned to cry – I was suspended in a space where time stood still, and I just stood there, waiting for the end.

After an agonizing time alone in the shelter, the adults returned. They had saved the house. An incendiary bomb had penetrated the third-floor ceiling and lodged on a floor beam next to my bed. They threw the burning furniture through the window and extinguished the flames with the equipment provided to us on each floor. Our training had paid off.

Next door, a young woman had been alone. She almost lost her mind. She banged on our basement door and screamed. After she was inside, she kept screaming, "When are they leaving? When are they leaving?" They left – finally, but I knew they would be back in the morning, the next day, or the day after.

Upstairs was a mess. The pungent odor of the fire had permeated everywhere. We went out to the street. Benzol tanks at the coking plant across the street were burning, several houses behind us in the next block were burning and the sky over downtown was as red as a blazing sunset. Fires were everywhere; one could have read a newspaper on the street that night. This raid had lasted only half an eternity. Our spirits were low. Our world was crumbling. It was difficult to go to sleep. We kept a candle burning.

An exploding bomb creates a powerful shock wave that travels through the ground faster than the resulting sound travels through the air. Two hours later, as I stood on the floor, my feet felt the first bomb of the next attack before I heard it. It did not take long before the convoy was on top of us and the pounding started again. The uncertainty of what will happen during the next few seconds turned into more torture. The sounds of death and destruction were all around us, and any moment could have been the end of us. I don't have the proper words to describe the mental anguish of those hours.

The raid continued, and through that ear-piercing noise we heard a person running through the street, beating on a metal pot to get attention and yelling, "Gas attack!" I knew about the use of gas during the Great War. I grabbed the mask, and with one continuous movement it was properly fitted on my face. I never felt any discomfort. With the right motivation, great obstacles can become minor hurdles. My motivation that night? I did not want to die. It had been a false alarm.

I had one more big scare that night. There was a heavy thump on the basement wall, the part that is about three feet above street level. Again. Mom covered us with her body. We looked at the wall expecting it to burst into the room and bury us, but nothing happened. After the raid ended, we went outside to see what damage had been done. It was like what had happened two hours earlier – only more so. The noise had come from the tail fin of the bomb that destroyed our neighbor's house; it had landed against our shelter wall.

A strong memory of that night is the odor of the upstairs fire. It stayed with me. Whenever I am in the vicinity of a burning building, that odor instantly awakens memories of October 14, 1944. I never stop to gawk – I had seen more fires than I could count. The streets were brightly lit from the many fires, and the sky had a red glow in several places. Our street was littered with debris from bombed out houses: bricks, roof tiles, glass, wooden beams, walls, pieces of furniture. Neighbors came into the street to see if their neighbors were still alive and to survey the damage.

THE NUMBERS BEHIND THE RAIDS

For many years I knew only the results of those three raids from personal experience. It took seventy years, thanks to the magic of the Internet, to discover the numbers attached to the events and the methods of those devastating air raids: *"Operation Hurricane,"* part of *"The Battle of the Ruhr."*

On that date, during the day raid, 957 RAF planes dropped 3,631 tons of high-explosives and 830 tons of incendiary devices. During the night, in two waves of 500 planes each, two hours apart, 4,000 tons of high-explosives and 500 tons of incendiary devices; 500,000 little fire bombs during the three raids; one for every man, woman, child, and pet in Duisburg. The death toll for the city on October 14th was 2,500.

That day, heroes were everywhere – in the air and on the ground: the bomber crews flying through a curtain of artillery shells and attacks by Luftwaffe fighters risking their lives to deliver their deadly loads – the civilians ignoring their own safety to fight fires and rescue victims – then there were the children, innocent and scared beyond belief – defenseless targets.

In his memoirs about those October 14th attacks, a British bomber pilot wrote, *"I flew my second sortie during the third raid. I saw the fires from forty miles away, before we crossed the Dutch border.*

Duisburg was burning. There are people down there – it was a horrible sight."

The next morning, my brother gave me an important moral lesson. A house across the street was ripped open through the middle from roof to street level. Half of the second-floor pantry was still there. On a shelf stood a glass jar of strawberries. As always, I was hungry. I said, "Let's get the strawberries." I could have climbed over the rubble to reach the jar. With a stern voice, Kurt said, "We can't do that, they do not belong to us!"

By any measure, the population of Duisburg underwent considerable physical and psychological suffering. It was a far cry from what happened in Cologne and Hamburg where uncontrolled fire storms flattened the towns and killed high numbers people in gruesome ways. Duisburgers had been fortune.

For the rest of our residency in our house, during the day we stayed in the Winkler's living room on the first floor listening to the radio for the next alarm. Our second-floor apartment was destroyed. All windows were broken, plaster fallen off walls and ceilings, and glass slivers on all surfaces. At night, we slept in the air raid shelter. We had many alarms day and night, some involved bombing others were just warnings.

The infra structure had fallen apart. The water system was heavily damaged, and we obtained water from fire engine pumpers positioned where water was still in the mains, although with low pressure. Half a block from us, a man had a small garden with an old-fashioned water pump. He refused to let the neighbors use it, but the authorities convinced him otherwise – in seconds.

The next three weeks were turbulent; alarms sounded many times each day; some were real, but most were false, but there was no way of predicting that. The Allied Army had advanced close to the Rhine River, and when their air support for the front was en route, the air defense system could never be sure about the intended target.

Gas, the main source for cooking fuel, was no longer available. Electricity came back later that day, or on the next. Soup kitchens were set up in schools to feed everybody. Usually we received a bowl of "one pot" or noodle soup with faint traces of meat.

Duisburg, once a lively city, had turned into death row. We have been convicted to death and were waiting for the day of random executions. The staccato of the explosions sounded like the death knell, and drumbeats accompanying the executioner's march to the gallows, and the drone of the passing planes were the dirge remembering the victims. At times the two sounded as one, and frequently either one would dominate the din. With the added noise of the antiaircraft guns, our World was filled with a spectacular sound that was augmented with the shock waves from the explosions. It was stereophonic sound at its best – and mental despair as its worst, but we survived.

ESCAPE FROM HELL

Finally, in early November, we received notice to gather only essential clothing and valuables to prepare for evacuation to a safe area. We went to the main railroad station to be taken somewhere, but we did not know where. I could not have cared less about our destination, because more than anything else, I wanted to get out of Duisburg.

The train was filled with women and children and a few old men. Most men and older teenagers had already left to serve in the army. The departure was delayed for several hours, because military trains had priority on the impaired rail system. I was scared. We had the usual false and real alarms. I did not want to get trapped in the train during an air raid. Finally, we moved out of the station; it was a huge relief. The trip was slow; we had many stops to let military trains pass.

Several times, the train stopped because of danger from strafing or an ongoing air raid in the next town. The alarms were given by displaying yellow flags at switching stations, the same way NASCAR drivers are alerted to a wreck on the track. The train stopped where the rails were depressed or partially hidden by soil embankments. These stops were extremely scary, because, again, we were helpless targets. There was no place to hide, no protective shelters.

Once, when we had stopped for a nearby raid, I heard the fighter planes shooting and winding their way through the sky. Fortunately, we had not been the target, but while I was trapped on the train, I did not know that.

A TEMPORARY HOME IN SAFETY

The trip ended in Tangerhutte, about two-hundred-and-fifty miles North from home and one-hundred miles West of Berlin. I don't recall if the trip lasted one day or two. The main thing was that we had escaped from the Ruhr Valley. By the way, seventy years later I learned about nicknames given to Duisburg by bomber crews: “Happy Valley” and “Valley of no Return,” because that area was heavily defended by Luftwaffe and eighty-eight-millimeter guns.

A four-mile ride by horse-drawn carriage took us to Weissewarte, a small farming community with cobblestone streets. We were assigned to the house of the Gueldenpfennig Family. They welcomed us with refreshments and baked goods served on the “good china.” Life in Weissewarte was peaceful. School was still in session until early Spring. Several families from home lived nearby, and with the local kids, we had lots of playmates. People in town were friendly toward us. They had compassion. They had been told what we had endured.

The Gueldenpfennig family had three members living on the farm: the patriarch, a very old man who did not smile and hardly talked. He took care of the horses and the cows and slept in the cow barn. Many years later, I understood why he did it: the barn was warm, and the sounds of cows’ stirring and chewing the cud had a calming effect.

The second member was a middle-aged man, the son of the old man. He took care of the daily farm chores. He, too, did not say much and always had a somber air about him. He was a multi-talented craftsman who could repair anything that was broken. It was fascinating to watch him at work.

Then there was Anna, the farmer's daughter, a beautiful woman in her twenties. She was friendly and interacted with the women. Life on the farm was a great way to heal some of the psychological wounds inflicted on us by the war, and most importantly, we were no longer threatened by the Allied air forces.

Just outside the village was a small landing grass strip. It was used to train pilots in dual-seat gliders. The first one I saw scared me. I looked toward the sky and saw this plane pass with dead silence. I felt like a little mouse that had just been spotted by an owl to become a meal. Gliders had been used since the early thirties to prepare pilots for the Luftwaffe before it was legal for Germany to fly motor planes. One of the 'Hitler Youth' attractions, a boy's organization like the Boy Scouts, but with ulterior purposes, had been the pleasure of building and flying gliders. I went to the air strip whenever I had a chance, because I enjoyed watching the graceful planes soar in the sky – they were no longer threatening as the first one had been, and they were flying silently; to me they now looked like huge birds – not bombers.

One day, a solo glider had crashed into the top of a tall tree. Rescuers set up tall ladders, tied the dazed pilot to guide ropes, and helped him down, step-by-step. The pilot's face was bloody, and he was obviously out of his wits from the crash. As soon as his feet hit the ground, an officer screamed at him and blamed him for destroying the aircraft. To me it looked like a cold-hearted reception right after the poor guy almost got killed.

Harvest time was work time. This was before "child labor" was invented. It also meant good eating. Bread was routinely baked in a communal oven in the center of the village; it was a stone structure that was heated with wood and then cleared of all embers. Rye bread went in first, when the heat was the highest; then came white bread, then cakes, and cookies. A loaf of bread was almost two feet in diameter, and it took a strong woman to hold it in her arm and run a knife halfway through it. That experience was excellent mental therapy. Adults had time to talk to each other, kids played, and the oven emitted a wonderful odor. The bake day lasted until late at night. It was such a good time. We were safe here, and Dad was safe in the hospital.

One new experience in the small village was the silence at night. Back home, I never heard silence at night – there was never silence at any time, day or night. The machinery from the factory emitted various sounds; air horns, steam whistles, and sirens sounded beginnings and ends of work shifts and lunch breaks at several plants; they were so regular that one could tell time by them. Tugboats on the river added their distinct whistle sounds, and the city traffic never stopped. A bell signaled the movements of the coal mine hoisting cages across the street. The city was alive with activities.

Here, it was quiet. Occasionally, the silence was punctuated by the rattle of wagon wheels on cobblestones, the clomping of horses' hoofs, and, especially during full moons, the chorus of dogs' barking as they talked to each other across town. There were no scary sounds; it was a peaceful place to live.

The Winter of 1944 was extremely harsh. I did not have proper clothing, and by the time I walked the three blocks to school, my chest was hurting from intense shivering. The arrival of kids was announced by the sound of their chattering teeth. Christmas was not as usual. We had no tree with decorations, no supplies to bake traditional cookies, and few gifts. We also had no air raids, and that was the best gift we received. Mom had baked three Bundt cakes, but since we did not have enough flour, she experimented and 'stretched' the dough with mashed potatoes. I can still see the cakes coming out of the oven; after a few seconds, it looked as if someone had pulled a plug – the cakes deflated to about half their original height.

1945 – THE END IS NEAR

The new year brought more changes. Everything used for normal living became scarcer. One advantage of living on the farm was the availability of basic foods, but clothing and shoes were impossible to find. Schools closed, and the buildings were used for military purposes.

A new phenomenon had appeared in the sky: huge convoys of airplanes; they grew bigger and came more often. The sky would gradually fill with condensation trails from thousands of engines, and the steady drone would last until they disappeared in the East: "Whooo, Whooo, Whooo." I did not know at that time that we were located under the air corridor between England and two prime targets: Berlin and Dresden.

That scene was overwhelming and difficult to describe. The size of the bomber force is almost beyond imagination; endless streams of four-engine planes – as many as one thousand. One thing we had not seen since the beginning of the war the presence of fighter plane escorts made possible with the arrival of the P-51's. Their single contrails were small and all over the sky as they scurried around the convoy.

Then there was the knowledge of the purpose and consequences of that massive military might. We knew, because we had experience with such actions. Planes started dropping millions of small aluminum foil strips. These strips rained on us and prompted rumors about their purpose. One story was that they were poisoned to kill kids who played with them. They were used to confuse German radar.

One sunny and quiet afternoon I stood in the farmyard when a British four-engine bomber appeared about two-hundred feet above me and headed directly toward the house. The plane flew very quietly and extremely slow. I froze in place and couldn't move – panic struck. I could plainly see a crew member inside the Plexiglas nose. It looked like a plane ready to land. Half a minute later it did. There was an explosion. The plane had crashed.

Another day, while we were playing on the street and pulling a little utility wagon, several solders walked through town; they carried a ten-foot-square wooden structure that looked like the roof of a house. It was part of a prop to practice house-to-house fighting. It looked heavy and demanded some effort, and they still had a long way to go. We offered our wagon; they were grateful to have that load off their feet. That was my only contribution to the war effort – it was not to kill – it was to provide comfort.

One afternoon I was using the outhouse when something approached the farm with a screaming sound I had never heard before. I pulled up my pants and stepped outside. I had taken too much time – it was gone. It was my first encounter with a jet plane, one of the wonder weapons that still promised victory until the last days of the war.

We knew by early April that the Americans were nearing. I don't remember how much of that information came over the radio. It would not have mattered, because we could hear the evidence of their advance: far away heavy caliber artillery fire. It started as a low distant rumble like thunder. The thunder kept getting louder every day. Our apprehension grew with the increase in gunfire. We didn't know what to expect from foreign troops.

Word spread that a supply train was burning about two miles from town. A caravan of people went out to see what could be salvaged. Several of the gondolas were on fire, and live ammunition had been strewn over a large area. It was a dangerous place. Teenagers set off hand grenades. There were a few soldiers in the crowd. One of them had lost his left arm. He had several "potato mashers," German hand grenades, strapped to his uniform, ready to fight to the end. We scoured the area to find something useful, but most of the stuff was ammunition; however, we did find one good item: a large aluminum pot, perhaps ten quarts. A year later, that was the only pot we had for cooking.

One day, a convoy of field gray trucks left the air base and headed East. About eight miles away was the Elbe River, the area where the Americans met the Russians. The next morning, the convoy returned to the base, because capture by the Russians was a bad option. The gun fire came closer, and soon we could identify mortars, and later machine guns.

THE START OF FOREIGN OCCUPATION

It was a sunny day, and we played in the street near our house. There was a small arms fire outside town. Suddenly, strange vehicles appeared; they were brown with white stars on the sides. First a jeep, then a tank, then lots of trucks.

"The Americans are here. The war is over!" Pure elation!

Town people lined the street to gawk. Soldiers had their guns trained on us. What did they see? Not enemies – just women, young children, and a few old men. I am certain they felt no threat: they just followed a procedure to safeguard against any unrecognized danger. Neither did I see enemies. I saw liberators. I felt no thread. I had no more fear. My feelings of elation were indescribable. The war was over. Six years of misery had ended – well, almost. The big war continued for three more weeks, but my war was over. Never again did I experience such an intense feeling of relief – this was the opposite of October fourteenth, 1944.

The convoy stopped to obtain the official town surrender from the mayor. In front of us was a truck with a negro soldier. We had never seen a person of color except in pictures from Africa. My mother, who never met a stranger, stepped toward the truck and asked the soldier, "Sind sie ein Neger?" "are you a Negro?" The answer, given in German, was profound, and came to mind in 1957, when I stood inside the Greyhound Bus Station in Virginia Beach: “Ich bin ein Amerikanisher Staatsbuerger.” “I am an American Citizen.”

We called Americans, “Ammis.” They did not mistreat us, but after things settled down, they evicted us from our houses to provide billets for their soldiers. The farm across the street had an enormous multi-level hay barn, and the second floor became our home for the next few weeks.

The town was secured, and the solders took time to enjoy some sporting activities to unwind. Volleyball, although I had never seen it, made sense and looked like fun, but there was a weird activity going on: a soldier with a big stick would hit a ball way down the street, and another one would catch it with a huge glove. He then would hit the ball with a big stick and send it back to the first one. What was that all about? We had received an abbreviated demonstration of a great American tradition: Baseball.

During the next few days, a seemingly endless stream of American soldier and equipment passed through town. The level of activities and noise had changed from one extreme to the other. At the Eastern end of town, the Ammis set up a huge gun. It came in several pieces pulled by massive tractors the size of tanks. The gun fired about once every half hour, and when it did, it shook the town. I hated that gun. It rattled my nerves every time, because it brought back memories of the bombing attacks.

When the crew preformed vehicle maintenance, Germans congregated to watch. The Ammis did not mind. One farmer picked up the emptied oil cans and drained every remaining drop. He accumulated quite a bit, one drop at a time, of something money could not buy: high quality lubricant for his equipment.

We boys roamed the countryside. We saw numerous burnt vehicles, dead horses, and all sorts of abandoned equipment. A favorite playground was the airfield. Several Ju-52 planes had been moved between trees at the edge of the woods; they were damaged enough to prevent any future flight, and they made fantastic objects for our imagination and provided hours of play time. There was also a large network of trenches for us to run through and fox holes to hide in.

Where American artillery had been positioned, we found sacks of discarded gunpowder, little pellets the size of a pencil tip eraser. We would fill a small artillery cartridge and light the charge with a match. The result would be a big flame followed by a short roar. Our gunnery experiments advanced. We filled a two-quart tin can with gunpowder, crimped the can's top so there was only a small opening left. We didn't know the gunpowder would burn differently in a confined space.

I placed the can on a board floating on the small pond inside the farm compound, lit the charge, and sent the float toward the pond center. This happened when a platoon of soldiers had the noon formation. Each piece of gunpowder was ejected from the can with a very loud bang; it sounded like a machine gun. The burning gunpowder flew in high arcs; it looked like a burning tree, a beautiful firework. Within seconds, a group of soldiers with drawn rifles came running around the corner. It was a big scare for me.

At dusk we saw a small plane in the distance; the crew of a truck-mounted fifty caliber quad-four machine gun saw it, too, and they let go a lengthy barrage of bullets. The tracers did not quite reach their target, but the visual action and the noise were impressive.

Soldiers were not allowed to talk to Germans: *Non-fraternization;* however, after dark, compliance was less than full We would gather at the back steps, my Mom, Anna, the two boys, and two or three Ammis. They carried on a light conversation with their limited knowledge of our language. There was some exchange of cigarettes and candy, which was strictly against military regulations. There was no breech of military security – it involved only strangers of two nations acting like real people – strangers trying to be friendly, and, of course, there was Anna.

While Dad was in the hospital, he had received orders to return to the front. "I can't fight; I have only one leg." The answer reflected the prevailing shortage of men, "You can sit in a tank." Fortunately, the Americans occupied the area a short time later. The hospital, filled with injured German soldiers, became a POW Camp; it was more of a formality than a physical act.

The Ammis set up a volleyball net and played. The Germans stood around the impromptu volleyball court to watch, but non-fraternization rules kept them apart. Americans lit cigarettes, then they would take one puff, and flick them toward the Germans so they could pick them off the ground. They had shared their cigarettes without violating orders. Although many ugly events took place during the war, on all sides, these gestures showed respect of the victors toward the vanquished. They were soldiers obligated to their duties, and they understood the predicament of the other side.

Around the end of the war, I saw a terribly sad scene: refugees expelled by the Russians. The stream of people seemed endless – women, children and very old men on foot and in horse-drawn carriages. They had few belongings, and much lack of food. The strain of their long trek showed on their faces, I read later that out of the fourteen million people expelled by the Russians from the Eastern territory two million perished during the trek. They were immigrants that had lost everything and no place to go except West.

I still see the images in my mind when I listen to *"Va Pensiero,"* the Hebrew Slaves' Chorus from Verdi's opera *Nabucco*. My wife asked me, "Why are you crying?" The image of such human suffering is overwhelming; you must have seen it to believe it, and when you have seen it, you can't forget it. I have seen it. I can't forget it. I am also reminded of my trek home – a small boy in a large stream of people, but with all the hardships I endured, I experienced nothing like those refugees from the East did. I was very lucky; I had it better than millions of others.

Eventually, in early May 1945, came this radio announcement, “Adolf Hitler is dead.” Then, on May 8th, we were told the war was over. I honestly believed there would be no more news broadcasts on the radio, because most of what I had heard was war-related. Well, I was wrong.

When people live in adverse conditions and are malnourished, there is great danger of disease outbreaks. The Allies started a campaign to prevent that. Everyone was subjected to a cursory medical exam followed by inoculations for the most common communicable diseases.

The Ammis moved equipment and troops into the former German air base. Our farmer had a field near the base, and we were out there gathering straw and helping where needed. Several children were there. Suddenly, we heard a loud whistle. An army pickup truck was passing with a soldier on the back waving at us. He had two hands-full of candy and tossed it into the street. We raced over the field; we were barefoot, and ignored the pain inflicted by stepping on the short stubs of wheat stems left from the harvest. We had not had candy for a long time. We were happy. The Ammis had been good to us during their short occupation. I believe by this time, we were back in our houses, it was nice to sleep in a regular clean bed again.

Then came a change of command; the British Army took over the territory. The “Tommis” were here. They were different than the Ammis. They did not mingle much with us and kept to themselves. They did not seem as happy and free-spirited as the Ammis, but they conducted themselves very properly and disciplined. To ease the strain of the foreign occupation and to show good will, they entertained us with close order drills and brass band concerts.

DAD'S HOMECOMING

In the early Summer of 1945, I experienced a deeply emotional event. Kurt and I were on the way from Weissewarte to Tangerhuette. We had received a letter from Dad; he had been discharged from the military hospital and was expected to arrive here by train later in the day. We took a little wagon, about four feet long with staked sides and four large spoked wheels, to carry his luggage home; it was a miniature copy of a typical farm wagon; it was as handy then as a pickup truck is today.

Either he had arrived early, or we had left late, our schedule was off, and Dad had already started to walk before we reached the railroad station. We saw him in the distance on the deserted road near the edge of the city limits, about a mile from the railroad station; he was the lone pedestrian. He was easy to spot. He had difficulty walking. As we got closer, I was shocked by what I saw. The Dad I remembered was handsome, like Fred Astaire. He looked proud. He could run like lightning, he was strong. He could lift both of us up under each arm and fly up the stairs to the porch, two steps at a time. He laughed a lot with us.

The events of the last six years had changed him. Two crutches had replaced his left leg that was blown to bits at Omaha Beach on D-Day, and he now needed his arms to walk. His gait was slowed by the small suitcase hanging by a belt from his neck; it contained his few possessions. With each step it swung like a pendulum and upset his balance. We met a stranger on that road.

Dad had lost a lot of weight. He wore his army uniform, which now looked several sizes too big; it hung loosely on him; that is all he had to wear. He had "de-Nazified" it by removing military insignia and replacing the buttons. His face was somber. He looked like a beaten man – old, thin, crippled, and hopeless. There was no laughter about him.

We hugged and expressed our happiness to be together again. We did not need the wagon after all to carry his luggage, because he did not have much – we needed it to carry Dad. He climbed into the wagon, and we pulled him home. The emotions during the trip home ran high. I was happy that we were there. Dad needed us. We brought him home in comfort the last four miles. Unlike our American Vietnam Veterans when they returned home, Dad was welcomed home. We did not talk much on the way home. What do you say to a stranger?

Mom waited for us at the edge of the village. I shall never forget the expression on her face when she saw her emaciated husband sitting in the wagon being pulled by his young children: it was disbelief. The man that used to carry his boys with ease was now carried by the same boys, grown older and stronger; their roles had been reversed.

For the first time in six years, we started living like a family again; it was difficult emotionally and economically. We had lost almost every material thing, and we faced an uncertain future, but we faced it together and without fear of death and persecution. We picked up the pieces and slugged our way through the post-war depression – we did it together.

LIFE AS A FAMILY

There wasn't any school until after we returned to our hometown; therefore, we had half a year of free time. That little wagon came in handy for gathering firewood for cooking and for the upcoming heating season; the forest warden had given us permission to pick whatever had fallen to the ground. Another activity was collecting mushrooms. Dad had received information from the forest warden and books on four types of safe mushrooms. These four were the only ones we picked.

Dad would sit against a tree trunk, in a comfortable position, and my brother and I would take the mushrooms to him to cut away all the inedible parts. At the farm, we placed our harvest on a sheet atop a flat barn roof to be dried by the sun. These activities not only helped fill the emotional void of the last six years, they also provided delicious and otherwise unobtainable food for many months.

Out in the woods, we experienced a peace we had not seen for years. We heard the rustling of leaves stirred by the wind, the chirping of birds, but we also heard a lot of silence – no guns – no planes – no sky filled with contrails – no bombs – life without fear, and Dad was with us. Those days were good therapy that was unavailable professionally, because there were not enough psychologists in the World to supply that service to the needy – to the population of Europe. On these lengthy trips we would sing, joke, and laugh a lot; it was wonderful.

Every day was play time. For toys we picked up the discarded military supplies, made imaginary vehicles out of cardboard boxes, and ran around the countryside. Occasionally, we would get into a bit of mischief. There was only one man we feared; he was blind. I don't know how he could find his way through the farm fields, but he did. He would appear out of nowhere and always scold us for having set fires. His nose never failed.

One game in the early days of the occupation was an enactment of a concurrent event. A few of us would be civilians living in the make-believe house represented by a farm wagon; others represented the American military forces. The "Americans" would come into the house of the "Germans" and, after a lengthy argument, evict the residents to provide billets for the soldiers. This happened when we were living in the hay loft, and it was one way to cope with the situation.

Our imaginations kept us busy and entertained all day. There was never a boring moment; all toys were of our own making; none needed batteries, and we got lots of physical exercise interacting with other children. I was lucky that I was able to spend the first half year after the war in the country. The only destruction we saw was military equipment. The shock of living in a destroyed neighborhood came later.

ENDURING THE PEACE

Germany Becomes Four Separate Occupied Countries

One morning, we looked out of the window and saw a disturbing sight: the Russians were here. The looked disorderly. They came on foot, bicycles, horseback, trucks, and whatever had wheels. They looked more like a caravan of Gypsies than a military force. There were many woman soldiers. The scene was reminiscent of the refugee trek, except these people were not looking for a new home in a strange country – they were the conquerors conquering more territory – Ivan. Germany had formally been divided into four occupation zones.

At various places Ivan erected huge propaganda poster with photos of Stalin and Lenin. These displays were reminiscent of the Nazi era when everything emphasized Nazi power and propaganda, except this time the subject was Russia, and the displays were larger than life. Ivan was also very controlling and watched what he did and where we wanted to go. Three officers occupied the annex to the main farmhouse, a small apartment reserved for the aging parents. They were friendly, especially with children. They had families and had not been home since the war started.

Several times the Russians erected a screen in the auditorium to show Russian movies. I did not like them, they were sad; however, I did like it when they marched through town: they sang traditional Russian folk music. Somewhere in the middle of the company would be a soloist singing as if he came from the finest opera house; then the entire company followed with a powerful chorus. The music was very beautiful, and people always waited until the company had passed.

We had been fortunate to be occupied by the civilized Russians from the Moscow area. The fighting troops from Mongolia and other undeveloped parts of Russia were tyrants, criminals by any interpretation of rules of war. Our Russian neighbors liked to hold parties with lots of alcohol. They were happy singing and dancing, and they shared their food with us. They were well-behaved and acted like friendly neighbors. Dad was no stranger to alcohol, but what the Russians drank was too powerful for him.

One late evening, we were standing on the back steps with two Russian soldiers, the same place where the Ammis had joined us, when something rustled in a bush next to the barn; it sounded like a small animal. One soldier took the carbine off his shoulders and fired several rounds in that direction. Another time, when a bunch of us kids were roaming through the woods, several Russian soldiers appeared maybe a quarter mile from us. One soldier raised his rifle and shot a few rounds to scare us. We dashed into the thick of the woods and never again saw the soldiers.

Compared to the Ammis and Tommis, the Russians were a wild bunch. One night, someone entered our room and went to sleep on our couch. He was a traveling Russian officer, who needed a place to stay. He didn't cause any problems, but it was a strange way to seek lodging. He was very polite. He ate several meals with us and then moved on.

RETURN TO NOTHING

Life became increasingly difficult; food got scarcer or was not available. Once we went to the only grocery store in town to purchase ¼ pound of brown sugar to make a snack with oatmeal. The customer who just finished her shopping heard our request, and she told the clerk that she forgot sugar. She got hers. When our turn came, there was no more sugar. Supplies were that scarce.

We had no hope to return home soon; the Russians would not let us go. In early Fall, Dad and Kurt hitchhiked by train to Duisburg. Part of the trip was on the side of a tank car; it was not an easy task for a one-legged man on crutches and an eleven-year-old boy. It was certainly dangerous. They had to sneak across the border through thick woods during the night. When they returned, they described what our town looked like: destruction everywhere. Our apartment house had been reduced to a small pile of rubble – nothing was left.

A month later, the evacuees from our Duisburg neighborhood hired a truck with a trailer. Dad had built a box to hold our belongings. It was the size of a small desk, and for wheels he used the rubber cushions used under artillery shells to protect them in transit. This was rubber turning on wood – hard to pull. We packed our few belongings and headed for the border that separated the Russian zone from the British. The Russians did not let us cross, and we were forced to return. On the way back, the truck's engine failed, and for the rest of the journey a farm tractor pulled us. It was fueled by a wood-fired gas generator, and it traveled very slowly.

In early December, the Allies had worked out a plan to repatriate us. The train finally came, and we boarded it. It was at least five hours before it left the station. Our coach had battle scars. A few windows were still intact, others were covered with plywood, still others were open holes. I don't remember the duration of the trip; it was slow and lengthy. Everywhere we went, we were part of a stream of nameless people going in the same direction – following a path of destruction trying to get back from where we came a year ago – home.

Every large town we passed had the same look: destruction, and the tracks leading into the station were filled with burned-out cars. It was a depressing sight, but nothing like what was awaiting us in the Ruhr Valley. The initial train trip ended somewhere in the Harz Mountains. We were housed in a castle from the Middle Ages. Our room was about twenty feet square, and we shared it with eighteen people. The floor was our bed. The Winter was harsh. Man-sized icicles hung from the flumes at the old water mills. The area was snow-covered; the scenery was beautiful.

At night I would look through the window facing a wide valley. There, in the distance, was a light – a new sight since the war had started; it made me cheerful. Christmas came. We had a little celebration. I can still hear, *Lo, how a rose E'er Blooming*. This was my first public Christmas celebration; it had an air of hope and peace about it.

There was an announcement, "Children under ten would receive fifty grams (almost two ounces) of chocolates." I qualified with age nine. In my family, if one had something, all four had something, because sharing was an important part of our survival. Once we had walked to the nearby town, and Dad found a carpenter who made us four plywood wheels that made pulling our box easier.

One disturbing event happened during our stay at the old castle: someone had stolen a woman's sewing machine. Two days later it was discovered outside the building; the thief had disassembled it, and now it was useless. He most probably wanted to transport it in his belongings, and somehow his plan did not work out.

We had one more short train trip to get to the border between East Germany and the British Zone. This time we stayed a few days in what looked like an internment camp constructed of crude wooden buildings surrounded by high barbed-wire fences. Again, the floor was our bed; it was wall-to-wall people.

We were told one evening that we were to leave the next day. Early in the morning, before dawn, we loaded onto a horse-drawn wagon and left for the border. The trip took at least an hour. On the way we passed an area where thousands of church bells were stored waiting to be melted down for ammunition. Some were a big as an automobile, others the size of a bucket. It was sad to see.

The morning was extremely cold. I stood in the corner of the wagon with luggage pinning my feet down. Our spirits ran high; we sang, joked, and laughed. When we reached the border, I jumped off the wagon and went down to the ground; my feet had been frost-bitten, and I was in great pain. The shoes I wore were at least two years old, and the big toes had already punched through the leather; they fit tightly and hindered blood circulation. We walked toward the border shack. Dad pulled the box with a make-shift harness; we boys pushed and steered it.

We left the Russian Zone and crossed into the British Zone. Absent were the propaganda posters. There was a feeling of relief as if a large weight had been lifted off our shoulders. We still had a long way to walk. We were part of a long stream of people. A British Army truck stopped near us, two soldiers jumped out, and asked Dad to get into the truck and took the box. They had smiles on their faces; they knew their good deed made our life easier. Soldiers respecting soldiers. Maybe it was payback for our helping the German soldiers carry the building prop. Their action lifted my spirits; I knew things were going to improve.

We arrived at our new quarters, a huge former German military barracks, and Dad was waiting for us. We passed though the check-in door. After we had our identification papers inspected, we were deloused with a blast of DDT up each sleeve and down the neck – then we received the meal ticket. The de-lousing procedure was routine at every transit camp; first came DDT, and only then came the meal ticket. We were assigned to a large squad room with simple cots. Kurt and I shared a cot; it was pure luxury.

We stayed there for several days until travel plans had been arranged. One must realize that thousands of displaced people were here waiting to go home, but the transportation system had been severely damaged, and travel had become difficult. Finally, we left.

The amount of destruction we encountered was beyond imagination. At times we watched stunned and in disbelief as the train passed through miles of destroyed gondolas and passenger cars that had been ripped apart as with a monstrous plow. It is hard to imagine the force it took to throw a fifty-ton steam engine off its tracks and lean it halfway atop a building.

At one time we had to walk between stations to another train, because the connecting bridges had been demolished. We had to cross several Bailey Bridges, prefabricated military bridges. German pedestrians were not allowed in the center; they had to walk on the side on two scaffolding boards with only two cables as safety rails. That was a horrible experience. I was claustrophobic, afraid of heights, afraid of loud noises. I was a mental wreck. Mom ignored the traffic rule and we went across the main section; that also made it easier to pull our box.

The closer we got to the Ruhr Valley, the greater the destruction became. I do not have words for the appearance of the cities. What I saw looked like a nightmare. No imagination could have depicted the utter chaos where people once lived. It looked as if someone had tried to eradicate the World.

We had to change trains one more time. All stations had the same appearance: physical destruction, hardly any sheltered areas, and overcrowded platforms with travelers surrounded by their few possessions. Some just sat there in a stupor. One young woman lost her mind and was screaming. Every station had attendants to help travelers, and that made it easy to get our box on and off trains. Finally, we reached Hamborn, four miles from our apartment, the closest one of the ten minor railroad station in Duisburg.

We slowly walked toward home; Dad pulling the box, with Kurt and I pushing and steering. The plywood wheels made it far easier than it was with the small rubber rollers. The closer we got to our neighborhood the greater was the destruction. Large clusters of buildings had been flattened, and hundreds were empty burned-out shells. Street cars were inoperative; the electric supply system was destroyed, and so where most of the cars. Sidewalks were covered with debris, but the centers of streets had been cleared with bulldozers to make them passable.

At Gate One to the factory, I saw a scene I had seen before – in 1941. I had taken my afternoon nap and awoke from a terrible nightmare. In my dream a bomb had destroyed a streetcar in front of Gate One. That is exactly what I saw five years later. This was the only time I had the dream before the fact. From now on I would have plenty of dreams based on experience, enough to disturb my sleep for many years.

When we came to within a quarter of a mile of our home, I did not recognize the area. Many houses on both sides of the street were reduced to rubble, and only the middle of the street was cleared to travel. I can't describe my overwhelming feelings. I had entered a surreal landscape. I felt utterly lost.

We arrived at what used to be our apartment house; it was once three stories high, but now it was reduced to a pile one story low. The three houses to our left matched ours. The damage was done in January1945; the coking plant across the street had been the official target, and our house was near that target. The reinforced ceiling of our shelter area had withstood the collapsing house, but a great danger would have come from the concussion of a large bomb which can be powerful enough to burst lungs. Fortunately, these houses were unoccupied at the time of the attack.

There we stood – stunned, speechless, homeless, wondering where to go and what to do. We saw no pedestrians, no familiar faces, and we were surrounded by destroyed buildings. The World I knew no longer existed; it was gradually obliterated during the last six years. The Allies' bombing had destroyed 60% of the homes, severely damaged a significant number of others, and incapacitated the city's infrastructure. There was an eerie silence – no sounds from traffic, the factories were silent, no bells from the coal mine tower, no horns from tugboats – the city was quiet and lifeless. It was dead. What now? We were hopeless. We had survi ved the shooting war, and we now faced another battle – the return to nothing and to a collapsed economy. We now faced a different war: surviving the peace.

Where could we go? While we had lost most material things, we still had one great asset: friends. On the other side of our block lived the Meurer family; they had a bakery, and their house was minimally damaged. They took us in. The customary German master bed is two joined single beds. My parents slept on the right side, the Meurers' on the left, we boys shared the sofa at the foot of the beds.

A NEW NORMAL

My paternal grandparents were bombed-out twice. My maternal grandparents, and two aunts lost everything once. My immediate family lost everything; however; we all gained something that did not come to full fruition until several years later – freedom.

The time had come to get our lives in order and try to live a normal life. That normal was established very quickly, and it lasted a long time. It was a normal, because it existed all over Germany. It was a normal, because it reflected the only available lifestyle. It was a new normal – ugly, painful, and inescapable.

The physical appearance of the cities had undergone a huge transformation: piles of rubble and burned-out shells where houses once stood. It was impossible to go anywhere without seeing the destruction. The housing shortage was acute. People lived in the remaining cavities of destroyed buildings, under bridge arches, and crammed into sub-divided apartments.

Lines at food stores were long. Little food was available. People wore ragged clothing and not enough of it. We were hungry and cold. Public transportation was barely functioning. Everywhere people were searching for people. On house walls and on signs placed on piles of bricks that used to be homes were thousands of notes asking about the whereabouts of family members.

That was the normal in 1946; it affected all people, and that made the burden easier to bear. Our family was no poorer than the average German family. We were in the same shape as our neighbors, which unfortunately, was normal for that time.

PICKING UP THE PIECES

The next six years were a struggle for survival that only gradually eased. The combat war had ended, and the Allies no longer concentrated on killing us, now they wanted to keep us alive.

Food reserves were scarce, production was at a low point, and the distribution channels were disrupted. There was barely enough food to avoid starvation, but not much more.

The amounts that we were given were allotted through "ration cards". There were no provisions for satisfying or healthful meals, just maximum limits for what we could have, and not for what we could purchase; the market could not supply even that little.

Normal food consumption is around 2,000 calories per person per day. In 1946, the ration cards allowed the purchase of only 1,500 calories, and in 1947, in the British Zone, that amount was reduced to 1,050 calories. That is what we could purchase but finding that much food was an impossible task. For some time, we lived on less than half the food intake required to be healthy. An added difficulty was the extremely harsh Winter of 1947.

The system of production and distribution was severely damaged, and it is a wonder that food even came to the stores. Where people could, they raised gardens – in vacant lots, in graveyards, and wherever vegetables could grow. We raised a garden behind our old apartment house and a rabbit in our basement. I remember the day when Dad killed it and prepared it for cooking. It was a sad day when we ate our pet. There was no problem with obesity, even as late as the early fifties.

In 1950, I was standing alone at the lower end of the Ruhr River Locks; it was a popular swimming place with a ladder to climb up to jump into the swirling water. A boat exited, and I heard one crew member tell the other, "Look; there is Mahatma Gandhi" He was referring to me. My ribs were clearly defined. By that time, we had better food and more of it, but no excess to develop a cushion around the bones.

Back to 1946; jobs were difficult to find. The only demand for workers came from coal mines; they offered special ration points to attract able men. A common saying at that time was: "With fatback you catch rats, and with points you catch coal miners."

At some time, we moved into a small room of our own. I think we stayed there about two or three months until we found an apartment. The generosity of the Meurer family made our lives livable at a time when we had little hope. We spent many evenings together playing board games, talking, joking, and laughing without fear about what was said, even telling Hitler jokes that would have landed us in jail just a year ago. There were no interruptions by alarms, and no police harassment because the lights shone through the open windows into the street. All our four immediate family members were home, just like it was before the war. Our social life was cheerful, but the economic conditions were horrible – far worse than during the war.

I don't remember when it was, but we gradually established contacts with our extended family. Two uncles lived within twenty miles from us. Both sets of grandparents were displaced and found new homes fifty miles from here. Dad's parents and another displaced family lived in a small house with the owners. They shared the kitchen, and access to the room of one family was through the bedroom of another. That was a common arrangement – it was normal, because housing was that scarce in Germany, and it took many years to ease that condition. Shelter was more important than privacy.

A NEW WEAPON – DEMOLITION

Henry Morgenthau had been U. S. Secretary of the Treasury. He had been responsible for war financing. After the war, he devised a plan to destroy all industries in the Ruhr that the air forces had missed, and prevent reconstruction, so that Germany would become an agricultural society and never be able to conduct another war.

The remaining German industrial capacity was gradually destroyed by moving functioning equipment to Russia, and by outright destruction of machinery too big to move or too damaged to repair.

The powers finally realized that Germany was being driven into unimaginable poverty, and the social climate would become like it was after the first war and be conducive to yet another one.

SCHOOLS OPEN AGAIN

I went back to school in 1946. I was extremely fortunate to have Miss Froehlich as fifth grade teacher. Her room had only one tiny windowpane, because the huge windows had fallen victims to bombs. Classrooms were damaged, cold, and overcrowded. We sat shoulder-to-shoulder on benches designed for lower grades, because we had about three times the normal number of pupils for a room. This school of three buildings was at one time two schools; the big building was for Catholics, and the two small ones were for Lutherans, but now we had to share the big one, because the others were substantially damaged.

Mrs. Froehlich was an outstanding teacher, and she cared about her kids. Several times a week, she would stay extra time to tutor four of us who had lived in other parts of Germany and lost about a year of education. She had great influence on my future. It is too late to thank her for her dedication, but is it the right time to tell teachers, "You have great influence over your pupils' lives; give your time generously; the kids need you."

Instructional material, i.e.: books, maps, paper, and pencils were totally inadequate. The Maps were from the *Great German Empire*, but Germany had gotten considerably smaller. History ended in 1933, because we did not discuss the years starting with Hitler's rise to power. To bring homework written on newspaper margins was better than nothing. Pencils were used to the last inch. To purchase notebooks required exchanging paper for recycling.

Good excuses for missing class were: "My shoes were at the cobbler," or, "My brother needed my shoes. "My two-year-old shoes had damaged my feet; I had developed ten hammer toes. Shoes were nowhere to be found. I switched from shoes to sandals – simple wooden boards with straps. That was not bad during Summer and Autumn, but Winter became a different story.

Schools started religious instructions again. The Catholics stayed in their classrooms, while we Lutherans walked to the Lutheran church a block from here. At times it was so cold in the unheated rooms that the pastor engaged us in some lively physical activity to get warm; that is all we would do. The school was six blocks from our house, and every block showed war damage. This ugly scenery was normal.

The Winter of 1946 was unpleasant. Our clothing was inadequate, and the lack of food added to our misery. Mom had converted part of a sweater to knitted gloves and socks. They felt good, but the open sandals soon canceled that feeling. Misery or not, Dad insisted on our going to school, because that is what kids must do – receive an education.

Schools offered cultural activities to add a hint of normalcy to our turbulent lives. I recall a forty-five-minute walk to an auditorium to see Shakespeare's play *As You like it.* Several classes attended. It was extremely cold. The walk was miserable, and it got worse when one of the sandal straps broke loose, and I had to drag the sandal with me by holding on to it with my toes. The snow eventually melted, but the cold slush made sure my feet stayed cold and made the rest of me miserable.

Another school trip was to a nearby movie theater that had survived the war. We watched Spencer Tracy as Father Flanagan in *Boys Town.* I have never forgotten those names.

ECONOMIC SURVIVAL

In mid-1946, we found an apartment on the third floor of a stately duplex villa on Kronstrasse, once occupied by the August Thyssen Steel Company president. The house had eleven-foot ceilings, marble steps, and one bathroom for each unit. Today, the building is on the National Historic Register, because the part-Jewish wife of the president had lived in the adjoining half. Her husband, Dr. Herzog, whose company was vital to the war effort, was unable to secure her freedom from the Theresienstadt Concentration Camp. She survived. Her daughter, Gerti Herzog, was denied education in a music school, because she was partly Jewish. After the war, she became an accomplished pianist. They were nice people.

For years I did not know what a Jew was. The first time I heard the word *Jew* was 1945, in Weissewarte. Mrs. Jacobs, an old lady lived near us. She was pleasant. She gave us candy on the trip in the horse-drawn buggy to the city. Some kids hollered, "Mrs. Jacobs is a Jew." I had no clue what they were talking about. One of my classmates was named Kohn. He talked about his dad's time in some camp and the severe physical abuse he received. By that time, I knew nothing about Concentration Camps; Germans did not want to talk about that part of their history.

Our first-floor neighbor, Mr. Becker, was superintendent at the steel mill, the second-floor neighbor, Mr. Krain, was the personnel director, and the top floor occupant, Dad, had been a waiter at the same factory. Because of the shortage, housing was no longer a reflection of job status.

We had a kitchen and a living/bedroom. To make the place livable, we carried many buckets of broken plaster and other debris, forty-five steps down and across the street to a bombed-out property. We did not always do it cheerfully, but we did it because Dad could not.

Gradually the apartment became a home. Friends gave my parents an old bed; Kurt and I had a cot from an air raid shelter. We fit on it like sardines in a can. When one turned, the other had to turn. Somewhere we found a kitchen table with four chairs. We had acquired a coal-burning kitchen stove and a "Warm Morning" heater for the living room. The problem lay in finding coal. We practically lived on top of coal mines, but the infra structure of Germany was broken, and the distribution of goods was impaired. We were lucky to have a pot to cook in, the one we rescued from the burning train in 1945.

Heating the apartment was difficult. My specialty was collecting wood for heating and cooking. There was plenty of it in the destroyed buildings. I stripped the plaster off wood lath and tore whatever I could away from the rubble. Sometimes our neighbor, a coal miner, would sell us a bucket of coal; that was a real luxury. Another source of fuel was the coal dust slurry from the coal washing process. The problem with it was the high-water content. Before the coal dust could burn, the water had to be boiled off with a generous fire from the wood. We managed.

We kids had assigned duties: mine was finding fuel, and Kurt's was standing countless hours in grocery lines at the stores to find food. Our meals were nutritionally incomplete, but that is all we had and not enough of it – another normal. At times we did not know what to fix for supper, because the cupboards were empty.

Freeze-dried vegetables made their appearance. They came in little white cardboard containers, and they tasted like little white cardboard containers, but they were food. Corn, potatoes, and cabbage kept us alive, but the body did not get enough nutrients to be healthy. I recall taking a bad fall on my knee. The resulting bloody contusion took over a month to heal. To fight the infection, we sprinkled sugar on the wound. Dad had learned that procedure to heal his leg in the military hospital. It is the same process as curing ham with either salt or sugar. We had nothing else.

When we boiled potatoes, most of the time we took the skin off after boiling, because it came off without the thick layer lost during paring. When we emptied the milk pitcher, we always rinsed it with water to get the last drop of skim milk. Mom did a great job trying to add flavor to our basic food. Mom did not let us put margarine or jelly on our bread slices. She always did it to use the minimum – there was not much to go around.

We kids fantasized about food. One big conversation subject was pancakes. Not just one or two; we dreamed and talked about stacks of pancakes a foot high. How much can there be to talk about? When you can't have any – a lot. It was a mental escape mechanism from hunger; temporary, it's true, and it did not feed our stomachs, but it certainly fed our imagination.

Macaroni was eaten in its simplest preparation: nothing on it except a light coating of margarine with a sprinkling of sugar – when we had it. When mom prepared cabbage, we boys got the core and chewed away every bit off it. I have told people that my mother had an ingredient that made everything taste good – hunger. Still today, I view careless wasting of food as a deliberate sin. Unless you have experienced prolonged lack of adequate food, you cannot fully appreciate the value of even simple meals as I still do. At the time of this writing, I had fixed two slices of toast for breakfast, but I did not have the appetite to eat both. I had strong feelings of guilt when I threw that extra slice into the garbage can. I still am not used to wasting food.

We cleaned up the basement where every renter had a storage room assigned. Mom had gone to Southern Germany to do some "hamstering." That practice involved bartering valuables for food. She had taken a gilded set of dessert spoons, forks, and knives and traded it for vegetables from a farm. I went to the bakery and got an extra loaf of white bread from our friends. We sat down, tore the loaf into three pieces and devoured it. We did not need butter or jelly; it was good by itself. We were hungry.

While Mom was gone, Dad found meat in a specialty store: horse meat. Mom did not like horse meat. Dad was a good cook; something he learned at his job. He prepared stuffed meat rolls, and we were lucky the meat came from a young horse; it was tender. When Mom returned from her arduous trip, she was surprised by the delicious meal. "Where did you find the beef?"

Food was a luxury. Much of our time was spent in lines at grocery stores, hours at a time, and many times there was nothing left when we reached the door. Our primary food was potatoes and corn, not Silver Queen or Seneca Chief; it was the same stuff used for animal feed, except it was ground into flour. Corn soup with corn dumplings was served often. It tasted especially good when Mom added celery leaves, if they were available. Potato soup was another favorite; that is all we had and not enough of it – a normal for that time.

School children were fortunate: they began receiving daily meals sponsored by UNICEF, a United Nations organization founded in 1946 to fight the famine in Europe. The Swedish government was heavily involved in it; hence we called the service *Sweden Meals*. After school we would wait on the street for the pickup truck to appear. It always was joyful sight. We would receive a spoonful of cod-liver oil and a bowl of delicious soup.

Around that time my mother made a statement that made absolutely no sense. Kurt and I were talking about the great pleasure we derived from the Sweden Meals. "Those Swedes, I have no use for them. Their mercenaries kept the Thirty-Year War going." What had a war from hundreds of years ago have to do with the humanitarian efforts of that same nation? Those ancient Swedish fighters had been dead a long time; I could not care less about them. Today's Swedes were feeding, me because I was hungry and could not get enough food from my own government. I liked the Swedes.

Another source of joy was the distribution of snack items: peanuts, chocolate, candy bars, all the things we either had never seen or were unavailable during the war. Once we received a large candy bar, something like a Mars bar. Our class had an extra one. The student who solved the following problem first would get it: "What is the sum of numbers from one to ten?" the teacher asked. I had often played with numbers and had the answer: "Fifty-five!" I shouted, and a half second later, Annegret Kascuba said it. She was a likable and very smart girl, but I beat her to it. Now I had two candy bars to take home to divide into four pieces. We always shared, while many of my classmates would eat their portions right then.

Mom had obtained a pair of military tent halves. With the help of Mrs. Krain's Singer sewing machine, Mom converted the tent material into a pair of shorts and a pair of short jackets reminiscent of the Eisenhower uniform. We wore them with pride. We wore camouflage clothing long before the hippies did in the sixties. Mom was good in making and converting clothing. Overcoats, shirts, pants, socks, gloves; she did it all. She had to, because these things were not yet on the market. We found a new type of sandals; an improvement over the wooden ones – they were made from worn-out tires.

DEATH RETURNED

Unfortunately, my parents started to bicker and argue. At a time when they should have been thankful for having survived the war, they started a new one, a war against each other. Their routines reminded me of the time when we had frequent air raids. The verbal battles kept escalating. Then there was harmony, but it did not last long. More shouting matches followed. Peace ensued, but the anticipation of the next round of fighting kept me on edge. Then came the worst.

One evening, Mom told me that she was going to turn on the gas in the kitchen and commit suicide. She opened the valve. I told my brother. He replied, "Don't bother me. Go to sleep." To shorten the story, Dad became aware of the situation, turned off the gas and stayed up with Mom. In retrospect, I think Mom used me to manipulate Dad; she had no intention to go through with the plan, and Kurt sensed it. This was an extremely cruel act. Again, I was faced with fears of abandonment and insecurity, the opposite of what I needed. Somehow the situation stabilized, but it had a devastating impact on my emotions. More than food and clothing, I needed love, security, and stability in my life, and for the remainder of my life in Germany, I never experienced a truly happy home. I believe that is one of the reasons I took frequent and extended bike excursions and then the ultimate one-way trip to America.

Fortunately, the closest I came to see the dead or dying was the burning bomber falling to Earth. Later, death came closer to home. I became aware of several people who could not cope with the post-war conditions. First it was a popular movie actress who ended her life; then there was a chemist from the mill who lived across the alley from us. Next was the butcher two blocks around the corner. The saddest one was Mr. Lange. He lived a block from us on the same street. I played often with his son who had a luxurious toy: a *Trix* model electric train. The family seemed to live an ideal life. They were attractive people, well-mannered, had a beautiful home, a high-paying job as open hearth superintendent in one of the big steel mills, and they seemed in control of everything. I was shocked when my friend's dad ended his life by jumping into a ladle of liquid steel. He could no longer cope with the stress of the prevailing conditions – he was an alcoholic.

My biggest fear, as was that of every child and parent, was Polio. Another illness that thrived among malnourished people in overcrowded living conditions was Tuberculosis. My classmate's brother succumbed to it; his funeral was the first one I attended.

JOY OF A RADIO

In early 1947, we had purchased a radio. We only had one bedroom with one bed for my parents, and a mattress on the floor for us boys. We were cold and hungry, and often we would go to bed early to stay warm and listen to the radio. The stations were government owned. Programming was varied: news, music, ear-plays, opera, public variety entertainment, and, yes, there was daily news without a war. Variety programs were divided into fifteen-minute segments, and my favorite of all was always the stand-up comedy.

Comedians could now make jokes about the Hitler era, current conditions in general, and food stories. One common joke usually started this way: "I have a new recipe: take one dozen eggs, . . ." The rest of the sentence was drowned out by hysterical laughter, minutes of laughter. What is so funny about a dozen eggs? Not a thing, but imagine finding a dozen eggs. The ration card allowed one egg per person per day, (it could have been less, but I don't remember) but the stores could not supply even this minimum.

We laughed more in those depressed years than in any year thereafter. We laughed not because the stories were funny; we laughed because laughter eased the pain, and dwelling on it would have made it worse. As life improved, especially during the early fifties, the subjects of humor gradually shifted from the economy to the occupation forces.

Some were an open expression of discontent with their presence, others poked fun of the Americans' habit to brag about their achievements.

Later in life I discovered that their bragging was not a way to appear better than others; I think it was just a sign of pride of American ingenuity and achievement. Just look at the conversion of American peace time production to war production. It was done in a short time and instrumental to winning the war. No other nation could have done that.

Occupation forces sooner or later wear out their welcome. This joke is indicative of that feeling, and a sign that life in Germany was getting better: A young German boy shines the shoes of a very tall American GI. He says, "Boy, if you can take the chewing gum out of my mouth without using a ladder, I shall take you with me to America." The boy replied, "Mister, if you can tie my shoelaces without bending over, we let you stay in Germany."

The second joke addresses the American tendency to brag. The Ammi approaches a boy in downtown Cologne. "Hey, boy," pointing at the huge railroad station, "how long did it take to build it?" "Mister, I think it took a year." "In America it would have taken six months." "Hey, boy, how long to build the bridge over the Rhine River?" "Mister, I believe it took only six months." "In America, we would have built it in six weeks." Pointing to the thousand-year-old cathedral, "Hey, boy, how long to build the church?" The boy acted surprised and said, "Oh, that wasn't here yesterday."

GIFTS FROM AMERICA

Back to 1947, somewhere around that time we established contact with Dad's brother, Uncle Kurt. He found us and his parents with the help of the Red Cross. As an American soldier, he had gone as far as Essen to find his parents, but he had been sent back to the States due to sickness.

At once Uncle Kurt started sending packages with clothing and food items. He would collect items in his neighborhood and supply us with wonderful things. Everything had to be used items, and a few strokes on the concrete sidewalk made any new shoe look used. My brother and I were the first boys in the city to wear Levi Jeans. We were the envy of our peers. Each package was a big surprise. Opening a Christmas package was nothing compared to opening a package from America. Every time we received one, we were overjoyed with the contents.

Two items from America got special attention. Uncle Kurt sent me a soccer ball, and I became a very popular playmate, because nobody else in my neighborhood had one. The second attention-getter, in 1949, was a Mackinaw coat. It seemed to have more colors in it than a rainbow. It stood out because no one else had anything with bright colors. It had arrived early in the morning while Dad was at work. By that time, I already had the old bicycle. That evening, I passed the streetcar with Dad in it on the way home. He wondered what sort of boy would wear such gaudy-colored clothing. "That is my son!" was his not-so-happy remark. This was the best coat I ever owned. It was wonderful, and by any measure it was pure luxury. It was very warm, and the size was ideal for bike riding. No one had anything nearly as flashy as what I was wearing. Henceforth, I became known in my extended neighborhood as "The Checkered One".

American clothing always got attention; it had modern style, often bright colors, and high quality. Germany just did not produce anything like that right after the war. For many years, much of available merchandise was advertised as "New from America."

At the post office, packages were checked for contents. I suspect that the officials were lenient, because they knew how needy we were. Once, two packs of Camel cigarettes went through undetected, and that made a huge difference in Dad's life. He sold the cigarettes for 280 Marks on the black market, and that was enough for a down-payment on his first artificial leg.

The black market was instrumental for the survival of the German population. If you had the money, you could buy almost everything: cigarettes 7 Marks each, butter 200 Marks, coffee, chocolate, watches, bicycle tires. It was a department store on foot.

DAD'S STRUGGLE

To make an artificial leg comfortable requires a considerable break-in period to toughen the stump. We went on walks with Dad, short ones at first. Eventually we would walk a far as downtown, the long way. The geometry was like a three-four-five triangle. We walked the three and four-mile legs, and sometimes some of the rest, but when the pain got unbearable, we would return home by streetcar. I know Dad suffered, I could see it in his face, but he never gave up; he was a tough man. He never complained, and I had high respect for his determination. That period of suffering made Dad's life easy for the remainder of his life.

Before Dad got his artificial leg, he was a night watchman in a scrap yard the size of several city blocks. He always came home well rested. Some streetcar main lines were operational again and had made it possible for him to travel to the job in the harbor area.

For some reason Dad lost that job, and he hunted for a new one. The only opening was for a public rest room attendant for the city. It was far cry from his trained profession, but it meant income to feed the family. He was ready to become a janitor, when an acquaintance told him about a bridge construction site on the other end of town, forty-five minutes away by streetcar. He was hired and received a simple title, "Hut Boy." He cleaned the construction barracks, made coffee, relayed messages; he was a gofer. He started doing other things, and before long he was in the tool room dispensing tools, keep them clean, and performing other simple tasks. He then started keeping time records for the payroll department. He never was a slacker and always did more than was expected of him, and he advanced within the company.

Often, when school let out early, I took the streetcar to his job site, for two reasons: firstly, the site was full of interesting activities; large bridge parts were hoisted by mostly manually operated derricks, and they were joined with red-hot rivets thrown through the air and caught by the riveter with a funnel-shaped bucket, and secondly, workers for this type of job received extra calories in the form of warm meals, mostly stew or soup, and there was always some left over for me.

In late 1947, I had dental problems. Our dentist had moved eight miles from here to the other side of downtown. The trip, normally thirty minutes long, took an hour and a half, because we had to cross temporary bridges on foot. To get a filling, the dentist needed silver. We were lucky to have Dad's Iron Cross Second Class, a silver medal similar to the Purple Heart, to provide the silver. The medal was made from "ersatz" silver – fake silver.

AMERICA'S MASSIVE AID

The American Government realized the conditions in Europe were horrible, and the situation could spawn another war, as it did after World War One. The Marshall Plan was born, and in 1948, it was extended to Germany. It aided in the reconstruction of the infrastructure. I still recall a huge sign at a construction site: “This power plant is constructed with Marshall Plan aid.”

Another great help and a sign of good will was the distribution of Care Packages funded by American private organizations. We received two of those packages. It contained food staples, chocolate, and a bar of soap. It was Ivory soap wrapped in paper with a picture of a boy sliding down a banister. At the bottom of the steps was the galvanized tub filled with water. That picture of the boy is still vividly in my mind. The soap we had, resembled an unfired clay brick with lye in it. Laundry detergent came in liquid form. People would take empty beer bottles to the store to be filled from a large barrel. That stuff was potent, and there were several cases of serious injuries and poisoning when people mistook the soap bottles for beer bottles.

In 1948, Germany got real money and disbanded the Allied currency. The economy now improved at an accelerated pace, and life in general improved. We now could purchase meals without ration stamps in restaurants. It also was no longer necessary to bring our own silverware or leave a five Mark deposit for using that of the restaurant.

It may have been in 1949, I am not sure, we had special discussions in school: Germany had been declared a sovereign nation again. The German language does not have an equivalent word to describe the meaning concisely; therefore we had to stumble over the English word without understanding its exact meaning. The three Western zones of Germany, with exception of the Russian sector, were a recognized nation again and no longer just a plot of land occupied by foreigners, although the occupation continued.

Destroyed buildings provided us with playgrounds; the cavities in the basements that used to be rooms made good hiding places. We kids did not realize the potential danger to us. Once I had just left the balcony of a half-standing house when it came crashing down to the street. That was a rude awakening, and I began to be more cautious about my playground selection.

The city had an estimated five million cubic meters of rubble from destroyed buildings. It had to be cleared sooner or later to begin reconstruction and because some of it was dangerous; the empty building shells were subject to collapsing. Narrow gauge tracks appeared in my neighborhood to transport the rubble to dump stations where it was transferred to trucks. A short trip to the harbor delivered the loads to barges destined for Holland. The Dutch people are skillful in reclaiming land. This rubble was no ordinary trash; it was hard-fired bricks and concrete. It was dumped to fill the area where the ocean and the Zuider Sea meet to separate the two.

A new occupation appeared after the war, and it was filled mostly by women: “Brick Knockers.” New building materials were scarce, but the bombing of houses had produced an abundance of used bricks. To make the bricks usable, the old mortar had to be removed, and that involved many women because much of the male population had been killed during the war.

In 1949, Dad’s construction company faltered, and he was offered a job working for the receiver, the financial caretaker of the default. The home office was about three miles from our house. His boss gave him a bicycle to make travel possible. One afternoon, Dad came home, smiling; the firm next door had a small railroad car filled with twenty tons of cement bags. He went back after supper and helped unload the car for twenty Marks. For a healthy man that is easy, but for a man with only one good leg it is a hard and painful job. Dad’s main concern was to support his family and earn extra money. I have said that my Dad was a lousy husband, but he was an excellent provider. In that respect, he was a good role model.

Around that time an old acquaintance had given Dad a bicycle frame. We scrounged and bought parts, and before long we had a second bicycle. I had just recently learned to ride on a friend’s child-sized bike, and now had a new freedom: travel. I gradually explored the town and saw the extent of destruction. It was a sobering experience. On weekends, Dad and I would take prolonged rides. Those were happy times – just Dad and I.

Eventually we assembled a third bicycle, and my brother could join us. Through the help of a neighbor we found a field where the farmer let us pick blackberries. It was a two-hour ride down and across the Rhine River. It was a source of food, and we had great fun riding together. On the way home, in a small village a carnival was in operation. I longed for a ten-cent ice cream cone. Dad did not have it – we were that poor. We also rode on the Autobahn, the German turnpike, because there was little automobile traffic.

Both sets of grandparents had resettled in Westphalia, about forty miles from my home. It was now easy for me to visit them in four hours by bicycle. In 1950, During one of those visits I had an inadvertent glimpse of my future. Grandfather had been a pattern maker at Krupp. After he settled in Frondenberg, he performed carpentry work in homes, and he became a well-known and respected handyman. I went to his work site; he was in the process of fitting an atrium door. I was impressed by his skills, but I had no idea that I would be doing similar work for a living after I lost my engineering job in 1992.

LIFE SLOWLY RETURNS TO NORMAL

Back to 1949; Everything improved: food, clothing, transportation, housing, and schools, there was hope for the future. Every improvement instilled an appreciation for its benefits; deprivation does that. I still feel that way, especially about food and clothing.

Dad's former boss, a WW-1 amputee, had started a manufacturing plant in Dusseldorf, about twenty-five miles from home. The plant worked the forty-eight-hour week in five days to reduce travel time. Dad had to get up early, around 5:00 a.m. He would turn on the radio. The Allies had a special radio program: "Learn English from the London Broadcasting Company." Its theme music was the overture "*Orpheus in Hades*," by Jacques Offenbach, a melody deeply ingrained in my memory. His trip included a thirty-minute streetcar ride to the main train station, a fifteen-minute train ride, and a final streetcar trip of about ten minutes.

This job paid a good salary; however, pay day came on the last day of the month, and during the first year, we had to finance twelve months' expenses with eleven months' income. Since several store owners knew us well, they let us charge purchases to an account and make final payments at the end of the month.

One Friday evening, Dad created a well-deserved embarrassment for two young women. At six-thirty, Dad starts the streetcar ride home at the railroad station, the end of the line. The first stop is downtown. The government allowed stores to be open till seven on Fridays. The car filled quickly, and all seats were taken. Two young women with shopping bags were standing near Dad. One turned to the other and said, with obvious intention for Dad to hear, "There are no more gentlemen who offer ladies a seat."

His response was totally unexpected and funny. Dad pulled up his left pant leg. It showed the sock fastened with a thumbtack to his wooden leg; he knocked his knuckle on the leg, and asked, "Lady, do you have one of these?" Their faces blushed, and they made their way deeper into the car.

Germany had an extraordinary number of invalids. I saw many every day. The most obvious ones had missing arms and legs. My barber had two artificial feet. The government had instituted a few rules that made life for invalids easier and showed respect for their sacrifice. Every employer was obligated to hire a certain number of invalids; I think it was five percent of total employment. The last two seats on the right side in every streetcar were reserved for invalids. Invalids had the right to enter the car before all others, and they could go to the front of a movie theater ticket line. One time a throng stormed the streetcar door and pushed Dad to the side. He inserted his crutch between the door handrails and stopped that nonsense. One legged men on crutches frequently used their folded-up empty pants leg for a shopping bag; a loaf of bread fit securely in that loop; that was a common sight.

During the school year, our class helped with building repairs; we formed a chain from the entrance to the attic, and we passed clay roofing tiles over our heads to the top, two at a time. There were not enough workers for the job, and everyone pitched in to get the job done. There were other unusual events, but that is long ago, and I don't remember everything.

Slowly, we progressed toward the old normal life. We accumulated a big bed and a few other furnishings. The first mattresses were bags made from tent material filled with hay. They were reasonably comfortable, but they contained thistles, and occasionally a prickly burr would poke through the sheet and cause sleep-robbing discomfort.

Rationing was gradually reduced, and availability of food and consumer goods improved. When the county fair opened half a mile from my house, we could buy ten-cent waffles without ration stamps. I stood in line for two hours. Kurt came to take me home. No way was I going home without the two waffles. That was real food for the family. The waffles went home to be shared.

BIG STEP TO ADULTHOOD

In 1951, I entered an apprenticeship program at the steel mill. It was tough. One of the trainers had returned from Russian POW camp. His criticism was merciless. He did not have any TLC for kids fourteen and fifteen years old. The training in the apprentice shop was thorough and extremely disciplined, and it instilled a work ethic that is rare to find in the twenty-first Century. I still benefit from the skills I learned in those early workdays. I survived that first year and went to my permanent post in the Telephone Department.

My new boss was an arrogant man: Herr von Koenig. When someone addressed him as "Herr Koenig," he insisted on "von Koenig." He never complimented us on our work, did not ask about our well being, and hardly gave the time of day, but the work was satisfying, and most of the older co-workers made the shop a pleasant place.

The main office was a different story. I worked for several weeks on one of the floors to install an elaborate phone system. Some of the young secretaries would not acknowledge my "Good Morning," and totally ignored my presence. Why? I was a blue-collar worker and beneath their social class. That stratification was common in the German society. I did my job. I did it well. Why should I be disrespected?

In 1952, Dad had helped me buy a four-speed bicycle. That bike opened a new World for me. It gave me a new freedom: travel far and in comfort, and it provided an escape from my unhappy family life. I explored my home state in ever increasing distances. I loved the feeling of independence and the joy of discovery. That bike gave me something else: speed.

My favorite ride was drafting a few inches behind the tailgate of a truck; in high gear and pedaling like mad made the landscape fly past me. It was exhilarating. Dangerous? Of course, it was, but not to me at that time. "Old people die," and I was young. That frequent exercise gave me an extremely strong heart (my cardiologist's statement) and helped me survive two heart attacks. I never went to dances and parties, and I did not chase girls; I chased trucks.

In 1956, my grandfather visited Uncle Kurt in Virginia Beach. As he stepped onto the *Superconstellation* plane, I felt a strong desire to follow him. America has always had a special attraction for me. I was impressed with Americans. That feeling started in 1945, when I met the American soldiers, and it was reinforced by what they did later: Marshall Plan, Care Packages, personal gifts and support, and the general information supplied by the news media. When grandfather returned, the accounts of his visit intensified my desire.

Soon thereafter, on a Monday morning, I was on my knees installing conduit in the pit of a "Hallden Shear" in the newly constructed cold roll mill. In the distance I saw Mr. Swarts, the

American construction superintendent of the American equipment. He did not know me; I was just one of many workers on his equipment. He stopped, extended his right hand toward me, smiled, and said in English, "Good morning. How do you do?" I was shocked. A total stranger cared for me more than my own boss. I was speechless. This was the defining moment in which I decided to immigrate to America. It was the first time I had feelings of social equality. I was not trying to be better than I was – not at all. I was touched by the respect I was shown and by the absence of social segregation. My goal was set.

AFTEREFFECTS

One subject I have avoided so far are the effects of the war on my mind; they are long-termed and never disappear: PTSD, *Post Traumatic Stress Disorder.* As a child, I did not know what it was, but I certainly felt the effects of it, and what happened was terrifying – it was like reliving the events.

The time came when there was no more danger. There was no one to harm me and no one to fear except the night. Many nights I did not want to go to sleep, because I knew what was going to happen: Deja vu. I like what Yogi Berra, the famous ball player called it: "It's Deja vu all over again," because the events replayed in my mind for many nights and many years, over and over again, and there was no escaping them. I am referring to nightmares. They are mental torture.

I now understand that the mind does not allow the body to die, and the protection is a sudden awakening before impending doom. I have awakened many times and felt physically and mentally exhausted from horrible dreams. Some were so realistic that after waking it would take a few seconds to realize that they were only dreams.

The immediate post-war years were terrible. In 1982, during my last visit home, Dad told me that we boys would scream at night. I never heard it, but I imagine why I did it. One recurring nightmare resembled a scene from the movie *Father of the Bride*. Spencer Tracy walks down a church aisle consisting of large black and white tiles. His legs started to sink deep into the tiles; he had to strain to pull his feet out for the next step.

I walked such a path many times in my dreams. I was trying to escape the danger, and it took all my energy to continue walking. Then the path ended suddenly, and I fell into nothingness only to be saved by awakening. I felt as though I was gasping for air when I awoke. Perhaps, that was the moment I screamed; I don't know. All I remember is the horrible feeling after waking. These dreams were physically exhausting, and they kept recurring. I hated them, especially the endings; the physical sensation of falling was all too real.

In another recurring dream, Kurt and I walked through the open countryside somewhere in a safe area. We pulled the little wagon I had mentioned earlier; it had our few possessions in it. Fighter planes appeared in the distance, and we raced toward the grove of trees to hide. The planes never shot at us, and we always made cover just in time. My parents were never in my dreams.

One more dream: The alarm sounds, and the planes are coming. I run outside, speed along the sidewalk on a wide stretch past my house. I flop my arms like wings. I become almost weightless. I am almost airborne, but I can't get off the ground. It is a terrible disappointment: I almost flew to safety.

There were many others, and most had the same theme: approaching danger, attempts to flee, no escape ever. These dreams lasted many years, but by 1961, they had almost disappeared. Fireworks still bother me a little today, but they no longer scare me. I am still easily disturbed by unusual noises coming from unknown sources.

In 1982, Col. Lambert, WW-1 pilot ace from Ironton, Ohio, and my family were standing in Ironton, when a small airplane took off in Wurtland, Kentucky, across the Ohio River. Lambert and I turned and looked to the sky; the others paid no attention to it. Why? A plane at one time was either friend or enemy, and checking it was an old habit. Jets never bothered me; they were new, and their sounds had no association with either war.

Occasionally Dad would tell us a few things about the war and his time in France. His stories were interesting, and I did not question any until years later. He was a machine gunner with an MG-42. It fired over 1,200 rounds a minute, and the Allies feared it. On D-Day, Dad faced the landing troops. "I never killed anyone." With that killing machine at his command, he could not have missed enemy soldiers even if had tried. I think he wanted to give the impression that he was a nice man and was not really a part of the Nazi clique, and he just could not kill. I knew better. Nice does not count in war; following orders does. His opinion about the American Rangers was, "They fight dirty." A retired Ranger at the VA Hospital told me, "If you fight clean – you are dead."

In 1982, on my last visit to Germany, the evening before returning to the U.S., we had a small gathering with Dad, a widowed aunt, the widow of his army buddy, and a few other family members. My aunt asked, "Erich, our spouses are dead, and you can now tell us; when you were in France, did you ever have a thing going with French women?" His emphatic reply was, "Of course not, I never did." I seized the moment and said, "Fathers and sons didn't do that – it was always the other people." Silence followed. This was the only time in my life I got to him, and I got to him good.

PREPARATION FOR A NEW LIFE

While surviving World War Two and the post-war years were a victory over adversity, I consider my next step an even greater victory. In 1956, I asked Uncle Kurt, Dad's brother, if he would be my sponsor for immigration to America; he agreed. I then contacted the American Consulate in Frankfurt, and right away I enrolled in an evening language school. My first teacher in a class of eighteen students was from South Africa; he spoke the Queens English. When positive papers came from Frankfurt, I switched to a personal instructor; he spoke a Texan American. Wow, what a drawl. Dad spoke some English, and together we practiced.

A letter came from Frankfurt: "Be here on March 28th." I went. We concluded the formalities, I signed several documents, and then I received the visa to immigrate to America – the ticket to the land of my dreams. During the next three weeks I was busy preparing with the Holland-America Line, sell my bike, say goodbye to relatives, friends and neighbors, and pack two small suitcases. Among the contents were four LP records, and one of them was "The New World Symphony."

On April 19th, Mom, Dad, and I traveled to Rotterdam. We went to the harbor; there she was; the "New Amsterdam", a magnificent Dutch ship that would carry me to America, to start my future – the future that I had chosen. It was a big step.

A side note: while I am writing this part of my story, I am listening to Antonin Dvorak's Symphony No. 9, "*The New World*." Every time I listen to it, I re-live the excitement of the ocean voyage and life in America. That melody reflects my mood in 1957. How did Mr. Dvorak know? He had traveled to America in 1893 and he too, was excited by what he experienced.

We said, "Goodbye." Dad left the ship early. I saw tears in his eyes. I did not know that I mattered that much to him. Mom was her usual self. Her biggest excitement came when she discovered the luxurious two-ply toilet paper in my cabin; in comparison, the stuff we had in Germany felt like sandpaper. The trip was wonderful. It made a nice transition to a new life. The morning of April 27th was foggy. We approached New York slowly. The Statue of Liberty welcomed me to my new land. To the average American, it is a nice statue. To an immigrant it is a welcome to a land of unequaled freedom and opportunity. It is a grand sight. There is nothing else like it to see.

A NEW WORLD

Life in America has exceeded all expectations, and I try, whenever appropriate, to tell Americans how good life is here, and, although I miss a few familiar things, that I have no desire to return to Germany. In my opinion, based on personal experiences, Americans are the most generous and forgiving people – and with more freedoms than any other.

Part of my judgment is influenced by the extreme living conditions under the dictatorship of Adolf Hitler. While such comparison may be biased and not reflect "normal" living standards, nevertheless, they expose what has happened, and, not totally unrealistically, warn us about what can happen to free people when they let their guards down and allow oppression to gradually enter their lives.

That process can be slow and concealed in the disguise of public welfare and national interest. It took quite few years before I became aware of the Second Amendment, and I was surprised by the reason for its enactment: protection against our own government.

You have read my story and learned what we children endured. My voice is small. The best contribution you can make in memory of the playmates I never knew, is the prevention of another war. Add your big voices, and together we may be loud enough for the World leaders to hear us and make peace their priority. We children get along well even if we speak different languages; that is our natural talent – until it is destroyed by adults.

Peace – let us keep it at all costs – it is less expensive than war and has a great rate of return on investment. Let us keep it with a government elected by the people and for the people. America, your people are fortunate.

EPILOGUE

April 27, 1957 is a pivotal date in my life, and in a sense, it is as important to me as May 14, 1936, when I started living outside my mother's womb. I experienced freshness every day, learning to adapt and follow the customs of my surroundings.

As I grew into adulthood, I became increasingly disenchanted with life in Germany. I had seen how American soldiers acted, the management style of Mr. Swarts, the lead engineer from the American manufacturer of the rolling mill, Care packages, the Marshall Plan, many gifts from my uncle's neighbors in Miami, and information from the news media. There was something different about Americans.

I went through the proper immigration process and learned basic English in night school. Immigration requires physical and mental health, skills to make a living, and a sponsor to take care of me so that I would not become a burden to America. During the Cold War it was essential that I had no connection to any organization promoting Communism. I met all qualification, and on March 28, 1957, I received my visa to America. I sold what few possessions I had, said "Goodbye" to family and friends, and went to Rotterdam to travel on the "New Amsterdam" to America.

The seven-day trip made a pleasant transition between the lifestyles of two continents, and on the morning of April 27, through a light fog, I saw the Statue of Liberty. To the average American, it is a nice statue of historical significance. To an immigrant, to me, it is a welcome sign as no other – I had cut the social umbilical cord and was about to engage in a different lifestyle.

I had mentioned in a Letter to the Editor of the Huntington, WV newspaper, that when a newborn American baby gets smacked on the behind, it is like an official declaration: "You are an American," and he experiences a good life and exercises freedoms unknown to a large population of the World, and you, as do most Americans, don't know how good you have it. For that reason, I want to illustrate a few things that struck me as notably different and touch on the advantages I have enjoyed in my new country.

Around noon on April 27, 1957 I stepped on American soil in Hoboken, New Jersey. From that moment on I was bombarded with new everything: sights, sounds, traffic, food, peoples' behavior, customs, climate – it was an avalanche of information and sensations.

My uncle's in-laws in the Catskills received me with open arms and provided a dinner I could not have imagined. The food supply in Germany had greatly improved, but it was nothing like here. Never had I seen such quantity and variety of dishes. The sight was overwhelming. These people had to be wealthy to put on such a spread. They were not. They were ordinary average workers who had access to incredibly inexpensive food.

After a few days, we drove to my new home in Virginia Beach, Virginia. America is so big that I wondered if we ever got there – especially at the snail's pace of 55 mph – but we did make it. We lived in a pleasant trailer park. Word got around about the German immigrant. On my walks through the park, complete strangers invited me into their homes to welcome me.

During the first two weeks I had no work, and I made frequent trips to the A&P Store. I had never seen so many varieties and quantities of food articles at such an unbelievably low price. I went there many times, just to walk through the aisles and look at the shelves. It was truly a wonderland.

Since I was an alien, I could not get a job with Bell Telephone where my aunt worked. My uncle's friend hired me as electrician because he knew of the comprehensive German training. To work, I had to drive a company vehicle. In Germany, the process of getting a driver's license is expensive and unnecessarily difficult. After two driving lessons we went to the police station for the test. Since I barely spoke English, my uncle sat in the back seat and translated the police officer's instructions. That could not happen back home. It took little time to understand that in America driving is a necessity.

Every evening, after supper, I had to read out loud a lengthy news paper article. It was tough. The pronunciation was difficult, and my tongue labored hard to produce sounds that resembled the intended words, but it was essential, and my vocabulary and understanding grew daily.

Something in the Greyhound Bus Station initiated my greatest disappointment with America: two signs on rest rooms, water fountains, and waiting rooms – "COLORED", "WHITE." What did "colored" mean? Uncle Kurt explained segregation and Jim Crow Law. I thought about what the black American GI said in 1945: "We are American citizens."

My job held no real future, so Uncle Kurt and my employer suggested that I should join the military service, and I did so on July 9, 1957. I first had to sign a "Declaration of Intention," an indication that I would seek citizenship at some future date. When I went to the courthouse, I was still covered with plaster dust from cutting holes for A/C ducts. I looked like a mess. The lady clerk received me warmly and treated me as if I was her most important customer. She understood the importance of that document for my future.

I was apprehensive about the immediate future, because of what the old German army was like and my limited language skills. An English test had one-hundred questions, but I understood only four. Basic training was in Fort Jackson, near Columbia, South Carolina. I was certain that I would die from the heat.

I was always late to execute commands, because I could neither understand the shouted words nor knew their meanings. I simply copied what the guy next to me did. I discovered that the purpose of the training was not to humiliate and degrade the recruits, but to develop skilled soldiers. At no time did a superior give me a hard time or ridicule my lack of understanding. Oh, we laughed a few times when my confusion was a hoot. My language skills improved. Unfortunately, I was conditioned to use the "F-bomb," and, when I went to town, I had to do some careful translating from German to Army English to proper English.

My technical skills got me into a very difficult radio school in New Jersey. I always carried a dictionary in my back pocket and spent many hours studying at night while my buddies played around and drank beer. I graduated, served eight months in Georgia, one year in Korea, and the last three months in Arizona. I had volunteered for three years and served where Uncle Sam sent me.

During my military service, I had two severe incidents of PTSD. I stood in New York City waiting for the traffic light to change. During the Cold War, the alarm sirens were tested every Saturday at noon, but I did not know that. The alarm was loud in the canyons of the skyscrapers – I felt as if I was going to have heart failure, my legs trembled, and I could not move. It took one second to realize what was happening; no one paid attention to the sirens except Private Staerker. It was a mental shock.

The second event took place in Fort Gordon, Georgia, during war games. I had volunteered to be an attacker; I was determined to get over my fears. During the skirmish the table was turned, and we became the targets. As the screaming enemy approached, I took off running. I panicked and was unable to stop. I followed a power line to the highway and got a ride from a passing car to the base gate. I called the company to get me. Unfortunately, no one checked into my problem. Technically, I was a deserter, and that alone should have prompted some action.

I was surprised to discover how many kids, especially the ones raised on farms, had been using firearms from an early age. I touched the first gun when I was twenty-one. It was the famous Garand M-1 rifle. I did not know until many years later the reason for the Second Amendment – another American freedom. During Hitler's time, ordinary citizens were not allowed to have guns.

In my spare time, I completed two correspondence courses and received a High School GED diploma. In Germany, high school had been out of the picture due to my social status. I was honorably discharged and went back to Virginia Beach.

On September 7, 1960, I experienced one of the highlights of my life: I became an American Citizen. The three years of military service rewarded me by getting the citizenship in three years instead of five. I was proud and happy. This was the reason I had left Germany.

I went to Winston-Salem to work and got married. My first wife thought I was very intelligent and should go to college. I had no clue what a college was. I only had an eight-grade education, but I took the S.A.T. test and scored high enough to be accepted at North Carolina State College. I used my savings to pay the $155.00 tuition for the first semester, but the second semester required a bank loan.

It was a tough life. The scholastic world was very difficult, especially in a new language. I had several part-time jobs, collected pop bottles to receive the two-cent refund, and lived at the margin of extreme poverty. I had flunked out due to poor grades, missed time due to major surgery, and I struggled to survive – but I never gave up!

College was a great opportunity which was out of reach in Germany. It took eight years of hard work and studies, and I was the first member of my family to graduate from a University. America is a land of opportunity, and I took the initiative to prepare for my goal and labor to meet the requirements to reach it. My social class did not get me there – determination and effort did – that is the American way – a form of freedom.

For the next twenty-two years I worked in several engineering positions at Armco Steel Company in Kentucky. I discovered very quickly that respect does not come with the job title – it is the result of effort and achievement. American society is not handicapped by old traditions that places people into certain niches. Americans can succeed in business – or fail. The freedom to try is available to all of those who are enterprising and willing to take risks. I had achieved the American dream: a good education, a well-paying job, a house, and a son. Life was good.

In October 2017, I had a sudden reminder of an event of 1945. I was on the way to my bank in Proctorville, Ohio, when I saw in the distance an old black man on crutches walking toward me on the left side of the road. He looked at passing cars as if he was hoping for a ride. Suddenly, I did not see a black man – I saw my Dad in 1945. Deja vu. I was determined to give him a lift on my return from the bank – that man was going to get a ride.

On my return I stopped and asked him to get into the car. Where did he need to go? "Across the bridge to Huntington to catch a bus home." His car was at a repair shop, and a friend was unable to get him. He had two miles of walking ahead of him. "I am Tony", he said, "what is your name?" "I'm Nick." We chatted, and I told him that I would take him all the way to his home 2 ½ miles from the bridge.

"Do you like the blues?" he asked. I told him that I did. He reached for his harmonica and produced this song, "I got stuck in Proctorville and could not get a ride, I got stuck in Proctorville and could not get a ride – along came Nick and picked me up with a smile."

That brief encounter with a stranger was very uplifting. I made his day by taking him to his home; it took no real effort on my part. He made my day by letting me give him the ride, and, most of all, by expressing his appreciation with the beautiful short melody – the blues as only a man who has experienced troubles can sing. This was real soul music – a "Thank you" from the heart.

I discovered through experience that Americans are the most generous and forgiving people, and they are blessed with many freedoms. The one big advantage in America is the diverse population. People from all over the World came here to make life better than it was in their "Old Country," and they have achieved that.

America is governed by ordinary people, and therefore by no means a perfect country, but it offers a life that is less burdened by economic, political, and social pressures and restrictions than any other part of the World. My experience with Americans has been positive.

I had joined a population that is friendly, helpful, and easy to befriend. With all the problems our nation faces, I know that America still is the greatest country. I am glad that I came here. I never had the slightest regrets. Thank you Americans – you have been good to me.

Made in the USA
Las Vegas, NV
15 November 2021

34464501R00092